ONE MAN'S RUSSIA

By the same author

Poetry
THE DROWNED SAILOR
THE SUBMERGED VILLAGE
A CORRECT COMPASSION
A SPRING JOURNEY
THE DESCENT INTO THE CAVE
THE PRODIGAL SON
REFUSAL TO CONFORM
JAPAN MARINE: A POEM SEQUENCE

Autobiography
THE ONLY CHILD
SORROWS, PASSIONS AND ALARMS

Travel
TOKYO
THESE HORNED ISLANDS: A JOURNAL OF JAPAN
TROPIC TEMPER: A MEMOIR OF MALAYA
BANGKOK
FILIPINESCAS

Novel
THE LOVE OF OTHERS

Drama
THE TRUE MISTERY OF THE NATIVITY
THE TRUE MISTERY OF THE PASSION
MOTHER COURAGE (Brecht)
THE PHYSICISTS (Dürrenmatt)
THE PRINCE OF HOMBURG (Kleist)

Translations
THE DARK CHILD (Camara Laye)
THE RADIANCE OF THE KING (Camara Laye)
MEMOIRS OF A DUTIFUL DAUGHTER (Simone de Beauvoir)
THE HEAVENLY MANDATE (Erwin Wickert)
THE TALES OF HOFFMANN
THE LITTLE MAN (Erich Kästner)
DAILY LIFE OF THE ETRUSCANS (Jacques Heurgon)
DAILY LIFE IN THE FRENCH REVOLUTION (Jean Robiquet)
etc. etc.

ONE MAN'S RUSSIA

James Kirkup

WITH EIGHT PAGES OF PLATES

PHOENIX HOUSE
LONDON

© Text and illustrations, James Kirkup, 1968
All rights reserved
Made in Great Britain
at the
Aldine Press · Letchworth · Herts
for
J. M. DENT & SONS LTD
Aldine House · Bedford Street · London
A Phoenix House publication
First published 1968

SBN: 460 07735 x

Contents

List of Illustrations	vii
Acknowledgments	viii
A Few Words of Introduction	ix
Author's Note	xii

PART ONE: A SEA CHANGE
YOKOHAMA-NAKHODKA-KHABAROVSK

1. A Voyage Across the Sea of Japan	1
2. Two Siberian Towns	13
3. On My Own in Khabarovsk	25
4. The Russian Shrug	33

PART TWO: THE TRANS-SIBERIAN RAILWAY
KHABAROVSK-IRKUTSK-MOSCOW

1. Across Siberia	41
2. The World Outside	49
3. On to Omsk	53
4. Moscow Time	62

PART THREE: HORRORSVILLE

1. Moscow Mules	75
2. An Atmosphere of Lenin's Tomb	82
3. Contrasts in the Capital	86
4. Moscow Mornings and Moscow Nights	94

PART FOUR: A GRADUAL DEPARTURE

1. Lovely Leningrad	105
2. The Real Capital of Russia	116
3. Out of Russia	128

PART FIVE: BACK TO TOKYO

1. The Journey Back	143
Epilogue	155
Index	157

Illustrations
between pages 68 and 69

Khabarovsk
The Amur beach
Komsomol Square. The small ads

The Trans-Siberian Railway
The platform at Novosibirsk
Bolshoi Circus acrobat. Girl gymnasts
Fruit drinks

Moscow
Soldiers at the Kremlin
A baker's shop. Theatre ticket kiosk
View from the Lenin Library

Leningrad
Peter the Great 'The Bronze Horseman'
The Neva

Stockholm
Hippies at the Concert House

The Trans-Siberian Railway
Footballer at Shimanovskaya

Acknowledgments

SOME passages in this book have already appeared in the magazine *English Course*, published by Eichosha Company in Tokyo.

Other passages were included in my regular broadcasts for NHK's 'English Hour' programme.

Permission to quote copyright material is gratefully acknowledged to Françoise Gilot and Carlton Lake, and McGraw-Hill Book Company for passages from *Life With Picasso*, published in Britain by Thomas Nelson & Sons Ltd; to William Collins, Sons & Co. Ltd for *Precocious Autobiography* by Evtushenko; to Faber & Faber Ltd and Oxford University Press, New York, for lines from 'Prayer Before Birth' from *Collected Poems* by Louis MacNeice; to Penguin Books Ltd for extracts from 'Mysteries' by Evtushenko, 'Bronze Horseman' by Pushkin, 'The Steppe' by Pasternak, 'Letter to my Mother' by Sergei Esenin, 'Verses about Sonechka' by Marina Tsvetaeva, from *The Penguin Book of Russian Verse*; lines from 'Birches' and 'Mowing' from *The Complete Poems of Robert Frost*, published in Britain by Jonathan Cape Ltd, Copyright 1916, 1934 by Holt, Rinehart & Winston, Inc. Copyright 1944, © 1962 by Robert Frost, are reprinted by permission of Holt, Rinehart & Winston, Inc., Publishers, New York.

A Few Words of Introduction

EVER since early childhood I have been fascinated by Russia. It was always my dream to make the long, slow trip on the Trans-Siberian Railway from Moscow to Vladivostok. In those childhood days, during geography lessons at school, I would pore over the map of Russia, spelling out and memorizing those curt-sounding names of towns—Minsk, Pskov, Perm, Omsk, Tomsk, Irkutsk. Little did I realize then that my first trip on the Trans-Siberian Railway would be made, not from Moscow and the West, but from Khabarovsk and the East, en route from Yokohama.

Like the realization of all long-awaited dreams, this was a sad disillusionment, though one full of strange moments of joy and adventure and terror and absurdity. I have a passionate admiration for the Russian people's achievements in the arts, in science and in the economic field. As a university student, most of my favourite authors were Russians—Chekhov, Turgenev, Mayakovsky, Gogol and Tolstoy. (I was thoroughly bored, and still am, by Dostoevsky.) I saw one of the last performances of the *Chauve Souris* Russian ballet just before World War II, and this left me with a lifelong love of ballet: indeed, for several years I trained as a ballet dancer in my spare time, and to this day I still have the big thighs and strong calves of a dancer disciplined by the movements of classical ballet. My experiences at the Bolshoi Ballet in Moscow and at the Kirov Ballet in Leningrad were to be among the high points of my Russian tour.

I also had a deep interest in Russian music. Though I did not like Tchaikovsky, except as the creator of wonderfully pretty and danceable ballet music, I adored the febrile artificialities of Scriabin. I studied the piano diligently and practised four hours every day until I could play some of his sparkling, melancholy gay *études*. I admired very much, as I still do, the vigorous, dynamic rhythms and native melodies of 'national' composers like Rimsky-Korsakov, Moussorgsky, Balakirev, Sokolov and Glazunov, and the work of their descendants, Stravinsky, Rachmaninov and Shostakovitch. I remember the last time I appeared on the ballet stage was when I was Gregory Fellow in Poetry at Leeds University. The city of Leeds was visited by a new ballet company which had somehow managed to acquire most of the scenery and costumes of Diaghilev's Ballet Russe: the new company called itself 'The Original Ballet Russe' and on its arrival in Leeds it applied to the various ballet schools and to the university to provide students as extras in its very grandiose production of *Coq d'Or*. I went along with some of my students and we were engaged, at ten shillings a night, with one matinée on Saturday, to walk on and stand at the back of the stage dressed as warriors and soldiers. I did not have to dance, but I held my lance very beautifully, so that its tip simply quivered with individuality.

All these things gave me a deep love of Russia. I suppose the picture I had formed in my mind was too ideal to be true. The truth is rarely pleasant, and the truth I discovered about Russia was a nasty shock to my poetic reveries about that great land.

To prepare myself for the journey I mastered the Cyrillic alphabet —this was a very valuable help, I was later to find. Then I learnt a little Russian grammar and various phrases which I thought might be useful. I bought a Russian dictionary and equipped myself with a large English map of Russia. This last item was also to prove most useful, particularly as a conversation-maker, for the Russians are always absolutely spellbound by maps, especially by maps of their own country published by another land. Many were the arguments and discussions my map started concerning names and positions of towns, borders, topography and so on.

I had been told that many Russians speak English, French and German. In fact I found very few who could speak them with any fluency. However, with my knowledge of these languages and my scraps of Russian I hoped to be able to make myself fairly well understood.

All the arrangements for my trip were made by the Japan Travel Bureau's Overseas Travel Section on the second floor of the main J.T.B. building in Marunouchi. The section dealing with Russia was very understaffed, and was virtually run by one person, friendly and helpful Toshiro Ito. Sometimes I had to wait hours before securing his attention, because there were so many Japanese wishing to take this cheap route to Europe. At that time I did not realize the enormous difficulties involved in travel to the U.S.S.R., and I had had no experience of one of the worst aspects of Russian life—Russian travel bureaux. Comparing J.T.B. with Russian travel bureaux, I can say that the

Japanese organization, despite serious understaffing, is incomparably more efficient (and what is more, kinder and more courteous) than the terrifyingly bad-tempered and inefficient equivalent in Russia. However, J.T.B. made one serious mistake in my case: I bought a round-trip ticket from Tokyo to London via Moscow and the Trans-Siberian Railway each way, but I was not provided with a re-entry permit for my return to Japan, something all foreign travel agents normally do for one automatically whenever one leaves Japan temporarily. This was to cause me and my university extraordinary difficulties and complications with the Immigration authorities at Yokohama when I returned to Japan. But I shall say more about this important matter at the end of my book.

I was to leave Yokohama for Russia early in July 1966, and though I began to make arrangements for my trip in February, I was told by J.T.B. that it would be rather difficult, as ships, air-lines, trains and hotels were already fully booked for the summer period, which is the busiest time for Japanese tourists. In addition, there was to be a mammoth British Trade Fair in Moscow during the month of July, and this had also restricted the number of available hotel rooms. My name was put on a long waiting list: if anyone cancelled his trip, I might have a chance to make the journey. About one month before I was hoping to leave I still had received no word, and was beginning to feel that it was all quite hopeless. Then suddenly I was notified that I could have a vacant berth if I did not mind travelling second class (what the Russians call 'hard class') on ship and train. For my return trip on the Trans-Siberian Railway I was offered 'soft class' accommodation—meaning an extremely comfortable compartment with only two berths. I accepted and paid for these conditions only to find, on my return journey, that there are in fact *no* 'soft class' accommodations on the Trans-Siberian Railway, and that though I had paid for first class I had to travel second class. (*And* I had to pay an extra twenty roubles in Moscow for some strange reason that was never explained to me by the angry fat woman looking after my tickets in the Hotel Ukraine.)

But all that was in the future, which, as the date of my departure, 7th July, approached, still seemed wonderfully rosy and full of rapturous promise of excitement and joy. This book is largely a description of my comic disillusionment.

Author's Note

LEST readers with no personal experience of life in the U.S.S.R. should imagine that my frequent references to Russian rudeness and gracelessness are exaggerated, I should like to point out that the Russians themselves are deeply concerned about this unpleasant aspect of the modern Russian character. At least *some* Russians are concerned, and lately Western newspapers have been reporting a campaign to instil the first principles of civilized behaviour and politeness into Moscow man. Vadim Kozhevnikov, a Soviet writer, wrote an article in the newspaper *Literaturnaya Gazeta* in which he urged his countrymen to 'cast aside their rudeness of morals and manners', and proposed not a new law outlawing discourtesy but basic training for everyone in the common graces of life, a training that would start in the kindergarten. Most Russians think that good manners are just softness, but there are some, like a woman factory engineer named Lyudmila Tarova, who wrote to *Komsomolskaya Pravda* that 'she would never spurn a man who helps me on with my coat or extends a helping hand when I am descending from a bus'. She goes on to assert that it is time for Russians to unlearn their ingrained bad manners. A book recently translated from the Czech, called *How to Behave,* has recently become a best-seller in Moscow, though this is no indication that the Russians will follow its advice. (Books sell well because they are commodities, and commodities in general are scarce.) Extracts from the book which have appeared in a large-circulation newspaper, *Nedelya*, gave some instructions on what would seem to us unnecessary old-world gallantries far removed from the quiet sincerity of true good manners. For example, a lady's hand should be kissed thus: 'Lightly hold only the tips of her fingers, give a charming bow and deposit a symbolical kiss.' Well, anyhow, that's better than nothing. . . .

PART ONE

A SEA CHANGE
Yokohama-Nakhodka-Khabarovsk

I

A VOYAGE ACROSS THE SEA OF JAPAN

FROM the outset I must make it quite clear to my readers that what I relate in this book is the absolute truth. There is nothing invented. I describe only those things that actually happened to me. I am sorry if the general pictures that emerge are unflattering to Russia, and I am sorry if my account distresses those Japanese who, like myself, have always been ardent socialists and devoted fans of Russia. But the truth must be stated.

While I was still in Tokyo, happy at the thought that this year I was going to escape from the long, hot, sticky Japanese summer, I made some entries in the notebook that was to accompany me all over Russia, and which was once nearly taken from me by Russian agents at Nakhodka. This is what I wrote:

'I leave Yokohama on board the *Baikal* for Nakhodka, Khabarovsk, Moscow and Leningrad on 7th July 1966. I feel it may be interesting to jot down now, before I leave, just what I expect to do and to see on my first visit to Soviet Russia.

'I have read two guides—Nagel's excellent *U.S.S.R.* and Fodor's *Guide to Europe,* which has a large section devoted to Russia. I have read three travel books in English: the Penguin edition of Laurens van der Post's *Journey into Russia,* Alan Sillitoe's Pan Books edition of *The Road to Volgograd* and Sally Belfrage's *A Room in Moscow*—a unique inside view of Russian student life, though it depicts a Russia of ten years ago. Nevertheless in many respects it is still up to date, and is one of the best introductions to Russian life by a modern author that I know. I have also re-read with great pleasure and interest Anthony Burgess's hilariously funny novel about Moscow, *Honey for the Bears*, and his other portrait of a totalitarian state, *A Clockwork Orange*. I am taking with me to read on the train Gogol's *Dead Souls*, Gorky's *Lower Depths* and Proust's *Sodome et Gomorrhe* in the second volume of the Pléiade edition, and the *Penguin Book of Russian Verse*.

'The books by Laurens van der Post, Alan Sillitoe and Sally Belfrage all have one thing in common—long discussions with obliging Russians about the Soviet system and the Communist way of life. All this I found tedious; I distrust politics and especially professional politicians, though this does not mean I am not politically conscious: indeed, perhaps I am too politically conscious for the comfort of certain career politicians. I am not a Communist, but I have humanitarian socialist-pacifist principles tempered by nihilism and anarchism. When I reach Russia I intend to ignore all political conversations and all attempts to 'indoctrinate' me. I think the Russians too must be heart-sick of politics.

'What do I want to do? I want to meet artists, writers, dancers, scientists, factory workers, students. I am not interested in ideologists and dialecticians, but in human beings, things and places. I hope to get acquainted with some animals and birds and also with soldiers, sailors and airmen. I am not in the least bit interested in the *stilyagi* (literally, 'style-hunters'), or any possible equivalents of British Mods and Rockers, for I wish to avoid all those chats about modern jazz and hippies, Beatles and 007 which I have had to put up with patiently for so long from my Japanese friends.

'I want to see ballet, opera, drama, a circus, a zoo, a school. I want to see a post office, a hospital, a fire station, a public convenience, a park, a collective farm, a library, a laundry. I want to see things as they are, and describe them as I see them, free from the rosy mists of idealism.

'I want to ask questions about marriage, education, abortion, birth control, Jews, religion, nuclear test bans, poets, drugs, homosexuality, prostitution, gambling and my great literary hero, the ex-Russian Vladimir Nabokov, the modern world's greatest master of literary English.

'Above all, as in Japan and any other foreign land, I just want to look, listen, experience and accept everything I see as normal and natural. I have no preconceived ideas. I do not expect to find much that is specifically or 'typically' Russian.

'One thing all books on Russia mention, and that is the concealed microphones and miniature television cameras in hotel rooms and public places. I have not the faintest idea whether this is true or not, but I shall try to find out. I shall pay particular attention to various suspect items of equipment in hotel rooms: radio and television sets [actually there are no television sets in Russian hotel rooms, I was to discover] and the bases of telephone receivers. I shall investigate the ventilators, where I am told microphones and television cameras are most frequently concealed.

'But this investigatory attitude sounds all too solemn for my liking —I prefer to take a flippant and mischievous approach to the subject. So whenever I enter a new hotel room I intend to shout at the top of my voice into whatever concealed microphone there may be: 'Hallo there! Here I am! Can you hear me? All right, listen away, you bastards!' Whereupon I shall reel off streams of filthy words in English and Japanese and in every other foreign language I know. (One of the first things I must do on the *Baikal* is to find a Russian who will teach me some dirty words: this, I have found, is always the best way to start gaining fluency in a modern language.)

'Then I can settle down to enjoy myself, knowing that "they" know I know "they" know I know. . . .

'The first thing I shall order on the ship will be a half-bottle of dry Russian champagne. [Unfortunately it was sweetish and not as cheap as I had hoped—about 720 yen for a half-bottle, twice as expensive as the much better Japanese brands like Hermes. Curiously enough, the dry champagne is cheaper than the sweet. Russian champagne bottles have those plastic corks which one finds nowadays on many cheap French and Australian champagnes.]

'I am sure I shall enjoy the boat trip, the long, leisurely train ride right across Siberia and European Russia; then Moscow—the Subway, the Bolshoi, the Kremlin, the Pushkin Museum, the food and drink; and Leningrad—the architecture, strolls by the Neva, the Hermitage Museum. . . .

'On my way back to Tokyo I shall visit, outside Moscow, Zagorsk with its fantastic monasteries and onion steeples, and Yasnaya Polyana. And outside Leningrad Pushkin (formerly Tsarskoyeselo) and that miniature Russian Versailles, Petrodvorets.'

These were the things I wrote, with a hopeful eye upon the future. Alas, many of my plans were never realized. A person travelling alone in Russia is at an awful disadvantage: in order to do most of the things

I had listed above, I should have had to be part of some important delegation, or of some well-arranged group tour. In a group one is protected and insulated against the worst extremes of the Russian temperament and Russian bureaucracy. I had no idea what spine-chilling rudeness was in store for me, for here, in the person of myself, a gentle, dreamy, fun-loving poet, the Russians were presented with a perfect target for their hard, materialist, bitter venom, and for their sadistic contempt. Ignorance is bliss, they say. I am thankful that, on my departure from my beloved Japan, I was completely unaware of the horrors in store for me.

On the morning of 7th July 1966 I took a taxi to Yokohama: the drive took one hour, and fortunately there was no traffic congestion, because at that early hour all the traffic was moving towards Tokyo. I left my bags at the customs and went to the Immigration block, a few steps away from the South Pier. Here the official stamped my passport and took my alien registration card. He asked me if I were coming back to Japan, and I said yes. I remember at the time he gave me rather a strange look, and I wondered if something were not in order. However, like most Japanese officials, he declined to comment on something not strictly within his own department, and allowed me to proceed to customs, where there were no formalities at all. Indeed all the way through Russia, Finland, Sweden, Denmark and England my bags were only opened once.

I went on board the *Baikal*, a fine-looking steamer with very modern lines, at nine-thirty to avoid the crush. I was nicely received by the staff in the 'Music Lounge', where I had to hand over my passport (as I had to do in every hotel I visited in Russia). A lady in pebble eyeglasses, looking at my passport and then stowing it away in some secret place, asked gratuitously if I were British, and requested the privilege of practising her English conversation on me 'some time next morning'. She was very sweet, with a smart hair style: however, I had no wish to be involved in conversation practice on a holiday, so I carefully avoided her throughout the voyage.

My second-class cabin was shared with two students of Tokyo University of Foreign Studies (Spanish Department) who spoke neither English nor Spanish. Nevertheless they were going to Spain, where presumably they would learn to speak the language. The other occupant of the four-berth cabin was an Iranian student studying books of very advanced-looking mathematics in Russian. He seemed to be planning some sort of astronautical career, though he looked more like a dreamy gazelle of a poet.

Up on deck, one hour before departure, coloured streamers began to be thrown, by the Japanese, from ship to shore and from shore to ship. Quite elderly men engaged in this typical Japanese pastime with childlike vivacity: how seriously and intensely, with what innocent absorption, they take this ritual of departure! Laughter, shrieks, cries, shouts, beaming smiles everywhere. Whenever someone misses a thrown *serpentine* it occasions gales of laughter, and there are more misses than hits, so the hilarity is unconfined. A band of students with a guitar-player is serenading—alas, with feeble Mexican pop numbers, not with the lovely Japanese folk-melodies—a pretty girl going to Paris. There are no tears, no emotional embracings, only laughter, laughter, laughter all the way. (How different was to be the return from Nakhodka!)

Everyone was being seen off by someone or by large groups of relatives and fellow workers. I searched the quayside for some well-known face: not one. I was apparently the only person on board who was *not* being seen off. The breeze-filled air between the shining white ship and the quay and the packed visitors' platform was soon webbed over with red, white, purple, green and yellow streamers. The ground was drifted with great rolls of the stuff, which women port workers kept clearing away, bundling up and packing into boxes for the incinerators.

The excitement mounted as departure time approached. All the Japanese seem to have a fixed determination to be linked to the shore by paper umbilical cords until the very last moment. Some are wearing wreaths of tangled streamers or plastic *leis* (not nearly so pretty) round their necks. If only there was someone *different,* I thought, someone who was *not* participating, someone standing apart, like myself, in brooding, romantic solitude! But the Japanese are great participators, and always feel a neurotic compulsion to be doing what everyone else is doing. Fixed, brilliant smiles on those Japanese faces indicate that, despite everything, this traditional ritual is something of a strain.

The passengers wearing a curious mixture of clothing: mountaineering breeches, sweaters and hobnailed boots; jeans and wooden *geta*; elderly ladies are in kimono; most men in business suitings, baggy and undistinguished; young girls all in Western outfits and honeymoon hats. Not a single male in the Japanese national costume. Few children, thank God.

From time to time, tinkle-bell chimes give out a saccharine theme from *Swan Lake*. Now and then the ship's siren gives a dismal hoot. A few Russian crew members look on this scene of childlike gaiety with faintly smiling condescension. Then the ship is edging away, prompt on 11 a.m., amid forests of waving hands. Gradually the streamers stretch, billow, strain and break, until they are hanging over the quayside piles like dollops of tinted spaghetti. For a while they form a loosely woven carpet round the boat, that waltzes in dirty foam to the strains of a lively *trepak*.

After the intense strain of seeing off the Japanese all retire to their cabins, collapse into their bunks and are sound asleep until lunch time at twelve-thirty. I do admire the sleepability of the Japanese. I found the two Japanese students already asleep when I went down to my cabin; the Iranian was studying his mathematics. (Russians are never put into cabins with non-Russians.)

I went up to the small, dull, unlighted second-class bar and had my first Russian drink—a bottle of champagne. One has to pay for each drink as it is served, as in Europe. The barmaid is a dear, matronly type. The stewardesses are very beefy, strong, *Betjemanesque,* with mechanical but charming, passionate smiles. Russian men's and women's figures seem bear-like and massive after the small-boned delicacy of most Japanese, and their clothes look shapeless. They have old-style hairdo's; men like 1946 spivs, with sideburns and pompadours, women tatty, bushy, coarse, stringy, wildly peroxided, beehivish, like bags of candy-floss over mean, sharp features.

My first lunch on board, like all the other meals I was to have, was a very poor affair. (Passengers in the first-class dining saloon get exactly the same food as the second-class passengers.) There were tiny pastry canapes topped with a little stale caviar, some bits of sliced cucumber and two small segments of tomato. Reddish cabbage soup with a spoonful of cream—is this the wonderful *bortsch* I've been hearing about in all those Russian novels? This was followed by a very greasy little hamburger with very greasy fried onions, raw cabbage and nice dry rice. Then four wizened, little, dark red, preserved cherries in a sort of large metal champagne glass filled with weak red cherry juice like watered blood. This is *kompot*—the Russian national dessert, like crème caramel in Spain—and it is revolting. Pale brown tasteless bread, roughly cut in jagged lumps. No butter. No tea, no coffee. A very hefty, middle-aged, motherly waitress; another has her hair dyed bright red. Their sharply upturned little noses contribute to the general sense of meanness. Just before I left Tokyo my osteopath had put me on a macrobiotic diet: I can see that by the end of this trip I must either break my diet or starve. I read somewhere that special diets can be arranged when travelling in Russia, but I could never see how that would be possible, for there was never any alternative choice of food on the ship or on the train.

I had a wonderfully good, long sleep in my quite comfortable, curtained berth. Next morning the time was advanced one hour. Dinner, alas, was a disaster: a few slices of dry sausage, cucumber and *daikon* followed by two slippery, squeaky *wieners* on either side of an enormous 'shaped' mound of cream potato. No fruit. No salad. A small cup of weak coffee. The food is not so much spartan as *mean*. I have the feeling that everything is calculated to the last shred of raw cabbage, though the motherly waitress did invite my neighbour, a doleful East German, to have another plateful of sausage and mash, which he eagerly accepted and wolfed down as if it were ambrosia or heavenly manna. I could only eat half a *wiener*, to the waitress's distress (feigned): she smoothed over the situation by pretending to assume I was feeling sick (I wasn't). The boat was lurching and rolling quite a bit as we sailed along the coast of northern Japan.

In the music room, with its hideous mural behind the piano, no sooner had I settled down to read and write than a screen was dropped from the ceiling and in came crowds of Russians and obedient, conforming Japanese to gaze in reverence at a very ancient travelogue, in loathsome colour, of the Crimea, dubbed with a mincing British male voice.

I escaped to the little bar, where I found two discontented-looking East Germans drinking Japanese beer, bottle after bottle of Sapporo, in complete silence. I had my favourite tipple, vodka and orange. I usually drink an American brand of vodka, the excellent, inexpensive *Samovar*, mixed with unsweetened orange juice: this creates a pleasantly dry long drink. By contrast, the Russian vodka had a curiously oily smell and a sweetish taste that took some getting used to. Russian vodka, at least in Japan, is more expensive than American or Japanese brands.

There are two shops on board, selling mainly souvenirs, but neither is open. It is impossible to buy a cup of coffee or some fruit. In the bar I purchased some dreadful stale Russian biscuits and poor chocolate to allay hunger's pangs a little.

At six-thirty this morning I was the only one on deck. We were still passing the coast of northern Japan, somewhere near the islands of Matsushima and Kinkazan. But it was a grey, misty dawn, and there was little to see. I waved to my sleeping friends in Sendai. The night before I had been in my bunk by 8 p.m. Over the loudspeaker—relayed to every part of the ship, even to one's own cabin, whether one likes it or not—had come an invitation to join an amateur talent contest next evening in the first-class lounge. Shortly after this came the announcement that there would be a dance that night in the music room. My two Japanese cabin companions, who were also already in their bunks, hurriedly dressed and dashed off to the dance, eager perhaps for the novelty of holding one of those strange, bulky Russian women in their arms.

On board are the two stars of the new Soviet film version of *War and Peace*, which I was to see later in Moscow. Harold Wilson also saw it one evening after the strains of the British Trade Fair in Moscow, and walked out half way: the film is enormously long and, though spectacular in an old-fashioned movie convention, immensely dull. The heroine, Natasha, played with great purity by Ludmila Saveryeva, was in real life a beatnik-looking girl chewing gum. The male star, Sergei Bondarchuk, looked worn and middle aged. They took no part in the social life of the ship.

I came to the conclusion that one should bring lots of provisions with one when travelling in Russia: towel, soap, spoon, plastic cup, Bovril, coffee powder, instant cream, sugar (the Russian sugar is like blocks of cement) and a large thermos of hot coffee. In fact I think it would be impossible to get hot water on this boat for making coffee or Bovril. One should also bring clothes hangers (there were none in my cabin's very tiny clothes closet) and lots to read. (There is a library, filled mainly with propaganda, lives of Lenin and Marx, but also containing some modern and classic Russian writings.) One should bring plenty to drink, especially fruit juice, which is scarce, and cans of food. It is essential to bring fruit too, though one should eat all this before docking at Nakhodka, as customs officials are very particular about allowing foreign fruit into Russia: one of the first things one is asked to declare is fresh fruit, presumably because there is so little and of such poor quality in the U.S.S.R. The lack of all these normal comforts and provisions is very odd in a rich land like Russia.

The library also contains many sets of chess, boxes of dominoes and also Japanese *go* and *shogi*, all of which are very popular. I never saw anyone playing cards. Scattered around the tables are free booklets and copies of the excellent magazine *Soviet Literature*, as well as coloured portraits of Lenin, with whose image I was to become so familiar everywhere I went. He looks like an intelligent bank manager; in some of his mass-produced statues, the forward-thrust, argumentative pose gives him the look of a shop steward at a strike meeting.

Breakfast again: three very tough slices of salami, apparently made of dried and compressed horsemeat. The tomato juice is diluted with water, but, as if to compensate, heavily sugared. (I have found the same kind of juice in hotels in Taiwan.) Watery coffee, lukewarm. A slab of heavy, greasy 'omelette' chopped from a huge lump of the stuff looking like a chunk of firewood. No jam. Again that dry, light brown, tasteless bread. A little pat of butter for each person. It all reminded me of an austerity breakfast in rationed, post-war England. A sense of poverty-stricken meanness about the portions and the way they are served.

Steep, narrow stairs. Slippery, highly polished floors, particularly in the second-class bar, where I often find my feet slithering to the roll of the ship. The henna-haired barmaid, her locks permed and covered with the ethereal sparkle of a 'jewelled' hair-net, is a dear, but always distant, always with a cautious look in her merry eyes. Every time I pay for a drink she attacks a big abacus with huge black or brown greasy-looking counters the size of ripe chestnuts arrayed on thick, curved wires. I heard many Japanese expressing surprise that the abacus, so well known in Japan and South-East Asia, should still be used in a progressive land like Russia.

I found myself speaking Japanese to this bar matron: she understands it better than my English or Russian. She has a sweet smile and, I'm sure, a warm heart. Most of the time she is surreptitiously reading a large hard-backed novel under the counter. Whenever any member of the crew comes in—even her intimate women friends with whom she has lengthy gossips—she quietly but quickly closes the book and covers it with a paper napkin.

Many Russians have deep-sunken, *cerné*, tired eyes, usually close together, and the tiredness gives a kind of bored, sophisticated distinction to their gaze, as if they had been indulging all their lives in unheard-of depravities. But this very charming barmaid's eyes were fresh and sparkling.

The woman in the first-class bar, which I sometimes visited, was quite different: a bad-tempered creature I'm sorry to say. I played some Beatles records on the juke-box in an atmosphere of stern disapproval emanating from the barmaid and her Russian passengers. ('We Can Work it Out' and 'Day Tripper' were the only Beatles numbers available, but there were also some good discs like 'Le Cœur qui Jazze', 'Taste of Honey', 'No Matter what Shape', 'Outcast', 'Inside —Looking Out', 'Don't let me be Misunderstood'. I felt that the last three mentioned expressed very well my own feelings on the *Baikal*. Then some Japanese girls came into the bar and tried to play something, but the machine went wrong; then two mechanics came and it worked again. Later I asked the barmaid for change for fifty yen (the juke-box cost twenty yen a disc), but she pretended to have no change: she just didn't want me to play any more decadent Western jazz. So I bought two twenty-yen bars of chocolate, gave a one-hundred yen note in payment and she was forced to give me one fifty-yen coin and one ten-yen coin as change: as I already had one ten-yen coin I was able to play another disc before lunch. To such pettiness I found myself stooping after two days in the company of Russians.

The shipboard party's awfulness: tuneless amateur girl singers trying to do 'Sweet Adeline' in close harmony. They were the daughters of some American missionary. I escaped from the packed and stuffy music salon, only to find that the concert was being broadcast all over the ship. I thought to find refuge in the second-class bar, but there too the music bawled out from an amplifier. As there were only the two morose East Germans drinking in silence at the bar, I ordered my drink, paid for it and carried it over to a table right underneath the amplifier. I reached up a hand and switched it off. At once there was consternation on the barmaid's face: she looked simply terrified. One of the East Germans rose from his bar stool, strode over to the amplifier and switched it on again, much louder than before. I let him do it. Why bother? He was a surly, unmannerly brute of a Kraut anyhow. After a few minutes the music inexplicably went faint, and the Kraut again strode back to my table from the bar and turned it up full volume again. It was ghastly. Not a word was exchanged. The nice barmaid was mopping her brow, which had gone white with fright. I expect the amplifier was 'bugged'. After a while the Krauts went out and the barmaid came over to my table and, smiling sweetly, turned the awful rubbish off. I kissed her hand.

July 9: Last night about eight o'clock we finally passed through the straits dividing the islands of Honshu and Hokkaido. These are called the Tsugaru Straits. Only after we had passed through these straits did the Japanese begin to relax and let themselves go a little. It was as if up to that moment they had felt they still had not left Japan. Young girls in their best dresses and those dreadful 'honeymoon' hats worn by prim Japanese young ladies came into the bar, flung off their hats, let their hair down, were invited to drink vodka neat by gruff Russian men with bold eyes; the girls played the juke-box and wiggled their neat little bottoms in time to the beat, as if hinting that they wanted to dance or be made love to by some wicked foreigner.

In the music room these Japanese girls, by now quite intoxicated, performed a very tame Japanese type of twist, an old-fashioned dance, but one which the Russians still seem to regard as the last word in daring. There was a very smarmy Japanese lounge lizard trying to teach the frug to an embarrassed, plump, blonde Soviet stewardess: I later saw them embracing in a dark corner of the deck.

About 3 a.m. the Japanese were still at it, singing Japanese folk-songs and Japanese versions of Russian folk-songs, while a number of middle-aged, moustached, wolfish-looking Georgians smiled wearily, but kept their baggy eyes on the abandoned Japanese chicks, hoping for a chance to make a kill. One or two of them, I noticed, were quite successful. In another place on the darkened deck, young Japanese men and women were openly kissing and embracing, some-thing which in Japan one sees only in summer time during beery evening pleasure trips on sordid steamers round filthy Tokyo Bay.

Next morning I saw Japanese young men trudging round the decks wearing old white sneakers with the backs trodden flat under their bare heels, transforming them thus into Japanese style slip-on slippers. I had often noticed this habit in Japan.

My first view of Russia: the dreary little port of Nakhodka: small, grey-misted hills behind quaysides lined with drab cargo boats. Grey day, grey, heavy sky. On some of the hills, dingy grey concrete apartment blocks. In the ship's library, an abandoned game of chess. The Japanese girls, wearing dark glasses and considerably hung-over, wearing their 'honeymoon' hats, are shaking hands with and giving their last goodbyes to their foreign dancing partners and drinking companions. I regret this sudden deterioration of the Japanese character as soon as Japan is left behind. And I miss Japan very much; my heart aches to be back there. There is a long wait before landing, so I spend the time in the bar (the first-class bar with the bad-tempered barmaid) drinking Kirin beer and reading, in Proust, a description of plum and cherry blossom, those favourite Japanese spring flowers, that made me yearn even more to be back, even in smoggy Tokyo:

... *ils étaient subitement peuplés et embellis par ces nouvelles venues arrivées de la veille et dont à travers les grillages on apercevait les belles robes blanches au coin des allées* ...

Though we had arrived in the harbour of Nakhodka about 4 p.m. we had a long wait for the very thorough customs visit. Eventually we all went and rested on our bunks. When the rather bored, eye-glassed, green-uniformed customs officer arrived in our cabin he was interested only in my suitcase, which was crammed with poems, typescripts and manuscript notebooks. I had read somewhere in the regulations that manuscripts and typescripts and 'literary works' had to be declared to customs officials before being allowed to enter the Soviet Union, but I had forgotten all about it. I had not the faintest idea that such a fuss would be made of my writings. The customs official could neither read nor speak English. First he called a young Red Army guard who was patrolling the corridor with a rifle: the Red Army guard came and stood over me: a grey-eyed, rosy-cheeked country youth whose facial expression was one of utter blankness. Then the purser was called, and I was able to explain to him that my writings were poems. (This was only partly true, and indeed one of my notebooks contained recent writings highly critical of Russian life on the *Baikal.*) The purser smiled and said 'All right'. (Russians speaking English *never* use that dreadful Americanism 'O.K.', which in my opinion is a great point in their favour.)

After that a grim, uniformed young woman not a bit like Garbo in *Ninotchka* stamped into the cabin and asked me sternly if I had any fresh fruit. I had one Japanese *mikan* which she confiscated: I later saw her eating it in a quiet corner below decks.

2

TWO SIBERIAN TOWNS

As the *Baikal* edged slowly towards the quayside at Nakhodka I stood at the rail and watched a small ferry carrying passengers from one side of the harbour to the other. The innocent Japanese, who wave and wave on the slightest provocation, like enthusiastic children, waved to the two Russian sailors and the group of headscarfed women on the ferry. The Russians did not wave back, but just looked stonily at us.

When we finally reached the quayside there were no welcoming banners and streamers; all was drab and deserted. Severe-looking young women in the Immigration Hall commanded us to change our money into roubles. It was all very intimidating and depressing.

Two young men, Intourist guides, came to meet us. One of them was short, plump, auburn-haired, vivacious, with a dazzlingly insincere smile—a sort of Russian Danny Kaye. Like many young Russians he had a receding hairline and the neck was shaved at the back in a 1945-ish 'square' look: at the front he had a kind of pompadour. I had first noticed this old-fashioned 'spiv' hair style, popular among the lower classes in England about twenty years ago, when watching performers and ring attendants of the Bolshoi Circus performing at the National Gymnasium at Sendagaya in Tokyo.

We were joined by a young lady Intourist guide and escorted on a bus trip round the town of Nakhodka. I was not much interested in seeing such an unattractive place, and said I would prefer to stay in the restaurant; however, I was firmly ushered into the bus with all the other passengers. The bus was small, old and cold. The girl told us about the origins of the town: the site had been discovered by seamen in distress during a storm. 'At zat time, it was yust a willage,' she explained in her charmingly coarse accent.

The town is quite nobly sited on an inlet among hills and sea mountains, but, with its glum buildings, broken roads and sad blocks of workers' flats, it gave an impression of unspeakable joylessness and dreariness. There was a large number of drunks staggering about the streets. The people looked simply brutish and uncouth, and I did not see a single smartly dressed person.

We were taken to see what is presumably the town's chief attraction —a seamen's 'International Institute', which was a sort of glorified Working Men's Club with a dilapidated, concrete, pseudo-classic exterior. The nicest place in it was a dim-lit bar where a few young seamen, served by two pretty young women, were drinking raw vodka chased down by beer. The two girls sported the familiar Russian female hairdo: a hairnetted beehive of badly bleached fuzz resembling a big bag of candy-floss. One seaman was wearing gold earrings. The drinkers paid no attention whatsoever to the foreign visitors: they were obviously under instructions not to fraternize. But in any case, as I was to find out later, most Russians are extremely reluctant to have anything to do with foreigners, even with those from Communist countries. This is one of the reasons why I was to meet so many lonely Negroes.

Free Communist literature was strewn around everywhere: magazines, newspapers, photographs of Lenin, pamphlets about Lenin and copies of Lenin's works in many languages. I could find nothing about or by Marx.

The foreign visitors, mostly Japanese, but including also a couple of Norwegians, a Swiss, two Britons, an American with a guitar (he couldn't play it) and, most extraordinary of all, a Californian bearded hippie with his long hair done up in a chignon on the nape of his dirty neck, seemed disappointed by this first view of the U.S.S.R. The hippie was wearing jeans and, on his unwashed feet, a pair of wooden Japanese *geta*; these drew no comments from the Japanese, who I could tell were feeling embarrassed by this ostentatious misuse of their native footwear. The hippie was a curious phenomenon who kept dogging my tracks all the way to Moscow; I later glimpsed him in the distance at Stockholm, where I was able to avoid him. We were the centre of an ugly scene in Khabarovsk which I shall describe later.

Then we were herded back into the bus and returned to the station and to our train which was to take us to Khabarovsk overnight. In the dining car I produced my meal coupons—how reminiscent these are of war-time rationing in Britain!—and was served an extremely poor meal by surly waitresses. I spoke to the permanently smiling Intourist young man about it and asked if it were not possible for me to buy something extra for dinner—some fresh fruit or chocolate.

His eyes sparkling, he exclaimed: 'So you think the meal was inadequate? You wish to make a complaint?' To this provocation I replied as he drew forth a notebook and wetted a pencil: 'I am not complaining. I simply want to get something more to eat. I'm still hungry.' 'May I have your name, please?' he asked. 'Certainly,' I answered and gave him my name card. 'And what is *your* name?' I inquired politely. 'I'll tell you later,' he said. 'I'm busy just now.' I never did find out his name, but I saw the same fulsome grinning personage in Khabarovsk again on my way back to Japan from Moscow. He pretended not to recognize me. (On that occasion the train was filled with a delegation of Japanese Communist and Socialist politicians, and so the food was much better, and served more amiably, though it was still inadequate and poor value for our coupons.) That first train meal was typical of Russian stinginess.

The view of Nakhodka Harbour as we steamed out of the station was splendid in the orange twilight: large, bulky cargo boats, lights burning all over their rigging, were sitting low on the high tide. Behind them lay some dark grey mountains, the mountains that at Khabarovsk form the border with Red Chinese Mongolia: they were impressively, poetically scarved in white cloud. One mountain was shaped like an almost perfect cone. 'Russian Fuji!' I heard one Japanese exclaim. Other Japanese laughed with delight when they saw two men fishing from the end of a pier. 'Just like in Japan!' they cried, for the Japanese are fascinated by fish and fishing. I felt glad that at last they had seen this glimpse of something human which they could relate to their own experience. But there were gasps of amazement when the train passed a woman guard patrolling freight trains with a rifle slung over her shoulder.

I was sharing a compartment with three other foreigners: as on the boat, no Russians were allowed to share sleepers with foreigners. Sexes were indiscriminately mixed. As I started climbing into my extremely high top bunk an old gentleman from Melbourne in a lower bunk whispered to me: 'Are there any women in with us?' I was able to assure him that we were all men in that compartment, at which he gave a sigh of relief and fell immediately into smiling, childlike sleep.

I felt rather unsafe on my high berth, for there was no ledge to prevent me from falling out; both mattress and pillow were hard and uncomfortable. Even worse was the continuous Russian music played at full blast from the amplifiers in each compartment—noble Russian baritones and squawking sopranos churning out patriotic ballads and national songs. After some investigation I discovered that this music can be turned off by using a knob placed above the window in the corridor: my smiling friend the Intourist guide saw me turning it down, and wagged his finger at me disapprovingly: 'Maybe you don't want to hear our beautiful Russian music, but others do. Your activity is not cultural.' Whereupon he turned up the volume again and walked away smiling after seeing me safely into my berth. I felt that already my Russian dossier must be rather large. The music was switched off towards midnight, but was restored next morning at six o'clock.

After taking two Seconals I slept, and awoke next morning to loud music and brilliant sun. After days of grey weather it was lovely to see blue and white skies, though the landscape through which we were travelling was uninteresting in the extreme. There were only two toilets to each carriage, with about forty people to a carriage. It was difficult to get into one of the toilets, but eventually I did, and began to shave. Almost at once there was agitated pounding on the door, but I went on shaving. (The water was cold and the toilet dirty.) After ten minutes I emerged spruce and fresh to find that the person who had been banging so furiously on the door was my former enemy on the *Baikal*, the horrid East German of the second-class bar. He gave me a look of sheer fury, but fortunately he appeared to be in desperate need of the toilet, so dashed straight in without speaking and slammed the door. The wash-basin had no plug: something I was to find everywhere in Russia. I had always thought the jokes we hear in the West about missing plugs in Russian baths and wash-basins must be malicious capitalist propaganda, but in fact it is perfectly true. I was to find that the gilt metal screw-top cap from a half-bottle flask of Old Parr Scotch whisky made an excellent bath and wash-basin plug. The toilets had no toilet paper and filthy roller towels.

Breakfast was not too bad, and I paid extra for two small cups of black coffee: no cream, and sugar like small lumps of cement took ages to dissolve. I had two small slices of hard cheese with the usual hunks of dry brown bread covered by a napkin to keep off the many flies. Two cold boiled eggs. From time to time the crash of falling crockery from the kitchen made everyone jump. One of the massive lady cooks was sitting on a chair at the end of the dining-car with a barely concealed expression of triumph on her crude face as she watched the helpless foreigners eating her wretched preparations. There was also a manageress, deliciously plump in black satin; with her sweet smile and curly perm she resembled an elderly Shirley

Temple. As far as I could see she served no purpose whatsoever, for she just sat there and smiled.

There was a ten-minute stop at Bikin. The big, stone-built, colour-washed station buildings with their vast halls reminded me of Spain. A peasant woman in a headscarf was selling wizened wild strawberries to passengers who brought their own sheets of newspaper and twisted them into cornet containers. The old woman refused to sell any to me because I did not have a piece of paper; when I just cupped my hands for some of the berries she blushed and hid them away under the counter.

We moved on again through a green and gently rolling landscape with ponds and rivers bordered by birch and willow; the blue mountains of Mongolia lay in the far distance. The scene reminded me rather of Hokkaido and Sweden. The rare houses were low, of wood, with painted window-frames and shutters and surrounded by what looked like honeysuckle hedges. The grass was brilliant with wild flowers, the profusion of wild flowers I was to see everywhere in Siberia that summer. Haymaking was in full swing, but it was all being done by hand, with scythes and sickles; I saw not one hay-cutting machine, not one tractor. The haystacks were round and pointed, in English style. There were huge fields of potatoes in flower. Round the houses I saw a few geese, cows and calves.

The general impression was of a flowering desolation, a fevered and brief reanimation of a vast and powerful giant of a land, on which a few tiny humans, dwarfed both by the land and the mighty sky, laboured in solitude and silence. The little villages set at great distances from one another were grey and sombre, without any colour save for an occasional painted window-frame. I happened to be reading Gorky, and found this passage which seemed to illustrate well enough the dullness of this region:

... In a town of the steppes where I found life exceedingly dull, the best and brightest spot was the cemetery. ...

(*Through Russia*)

Just after noon we began to approach Khabarovsk. We passed by timber-mills and saw-mills and vast yards stacked with logs and tree trunks. We crossed rivers jammed with unmoving piles of timber. Other yards held mounds of wooden barrels. Small wooden bridges over streams extended into elevated catwalks across the fields, joining house and road; these were presumably to enable the occupants of remote houses to reach the nearest road in the deep snowfalls of the Siberian winter.

A solitary reaper, a tall young man standing in a field of wild flowers, his glittering scythe like a great wing, a metal extension of his right arm and shoulder. He stands in an easy, graceful posture, left hand on hip, suntanned wrist illuminated by a metal wrist-watch and strap. A red handkerchief tied over his head gives him the appearance of a lazy buccaneer. But his face is expressionless as he watches our train slide by. By now none of the Japanese at the train windows bother to wave to him; they no longer wave to anyone, for they know there will be no response.

Beside a vast river, the Amur, stand modest one-storey whitewashed cottages with brown-painted window-frames, each house shaded by four or five silver birches—Russia's most common and favourite tree—that cast a constant twinkling pattern of shade on the sunny walls. The roofs, as in Sweden and Hokkaido, are steep—a forty-five degree angle at the roof point—to bear better the long winter's tons of ice and snow.

I've just realized that it's a Sunday: one would never know it. Riding into Khabarovsk I have a feeling of excitement and expectancy at my first sight of a large Siberian city. I see factory after factory whose roofs and smoke-stacks are surmounted by huge red stars. There are many blocks of workers' apartments, their high gable-ends decorated with crude propaganda murals of heroic Soviet men and women all showing set, tense, blank faces of abstract handsomeness, all engaged in symbolic work with tractors or machines or holding simplified sheaves of corn like the Co-op sign. On the outskirts of the city these factories and apartments are interspersed by fields, little valleys of vegetables, small wooden houses and silver birch groves with nanny-goats grazing in their shade. Nearer the centre, lost among all the big blocks, a tiny church with one grey metal-plated turnip dome, one modest steeple whose tip is lost among swaying birches: it looks very subdued, very quiet, very small. A tilted cross on a leaning spire of weather-beaten wood.

We were met by fresh Intourist guides at Khabarovsk station, where a primitive bus whisked us away round the vainglorious modern statue of the founder of the city, the explorer Khabarov, garbed in furs, astride an enormous 'rusticated' plinth. There were people about, but the streets, even round the station, looked empty after Japan. There was very little traffic—mostly trucks and buses, and only very occasionally a private car. The bus bumped us round the wide plaza of lawns and flower beds and fountains called Lenin Square, where the usual aggressively forward-leaning statue of Lenin, in a cloth cap, reared up in front of the drab façade of the General Hospital. Then we rolled down the main street, a wide boulevard lined with State department stores and offices interspersed with a few cafés and cinemas and the city's one 'live' theatre. It is a street of noble proportions leading down to a pleasure park and the beaches along the Amur River; but there was little sense of gaiety and movement in the thin crowds, and a feeling of stingy poverty in the undressed or almost empty windows. The biggest crowds were round ice-cream carts, where scores of people were always queuing for Russia's favourite luxury. There were also little groups round carts selling small-beer called *kvass*, an insipid drink made from fermented black bread. The name was familiar to me from my readings of Russian novelists: judging from the way they write about it I had supposed it to be some kind of divine nectar, but it is quite the opposite. Other small crowds stood around fruit juice stalls: these natural fruit juices —plum, tomato, cherry—were among the cheapest and most delightful drinks to be had in Russia. The people themselves were undistinguished, even though in their Sunday best, the girls and women in cheap cotton dresses and head-scarves and sling-backed shoes, the men in drab, shapeless trousers, open-necked rayon shirts and clumsy leather or imitation leather sandals. Only the children danced along and sometimes seemed carefree and happy.

We were taken first to the Far Eastern Hotel on this main street— known as Karl Marx Street—and here we waited half an hour in the entrance hall while the Intourist guides fussed about. Eventually we were told there were no rooms for us there, and one American lady with two young daughters began to have hysterics: 'But I was *told*, I was *promised* there would be rooms for us here . . . I never saw such bad organization and downright inefficiency . . .' and so on and so on.

We were escorted back into the bus (we had been told we must not leave the hotel until we had registered) and driven back up Karl Marx Street to Lenin Square, where there stands Khabarovsk's other hotel, the Central Hotel (and restaurant, such as it is, to which I shall return later). Here it took at least one hour to check in. Our passports were taken and held by a Gorgon-like lady at the reception desk. I managed to insist on having a single room all to myself, but the others all had to share, excepting an elderly Swede who refused absolutely to share a room with the rather sweet, vaguely saintly, naïve American hippie with the curly beard and the long, curly, dirty hair tied in a bun at the back of his neck with a much-used rubber band. He carried an embroidered Burmese monk's begging satchel slung from one shoulder. He was wearing far-out, 'granny-style' sun-glasses with small square black lenses in tin frames, right out of *Dr Mabuse*. I felt rather glad to see this hippie in prim, bourgeois Khabarovsk. But I could never quite make up my mind about him. He had lived in India and Burma as well as in Japan and seemed to be evolving a religion all his own. In the end I decided he was a phoney, not sensitive or saintly at all, and thick-skinned and stupid rather than brave and wise. Nevertheless a good phoney.

There was a stodgy provincial Sunday atmosphere of solid respectability and cautious prosperity. Though the cafés and cinemas and shops were full, the lack of traffic on the streets gave the city an unreal look. The few small privately owned Zim cars lacked all style and elegance, and the battered taxis were rare. Over it all lounged the statue of Lenin with his false-looking pointed beard, strutting in a self-consciously rhetorical pose, cloth cap set straight on his head, right hand in trouser pocket, left hand grasping left lapel. How could anyone believe in an absurd figure like that? Indeed I remarked that the passers-by took no notice at all of this grandiloquent statue: it was perhaps so big and so awful, one couldn't help overlooking it.

After lunch, which I obtained with the greatest difficulty from the angry young waitresses in the hotel restaurant (I soon found out that the cold mixed meat dish is the best value, and the least inedible), a lady guide from Intourist invited me to take a taxi tour of the city. 'Your companion', she said, with a smile of would-be complicity to which I refused to react, 'will be the American gentleman with the Japanese sandals and the beard.' Apparently everyone else had refused to go with him. This gave me a sudden urge to see the sights with Mr Everly—such was his name—as I wanted to observe the reactions of the staid burghers of Khabarovsk to such an outlandish figure. He was, I felt sure, affronting modern Russia in a way I had wanted to do ever since boarding the *Baikal*.

It took nearly two hours to catch the waitress's eye, order, wait for, eat and pay for lunch. The lady guide waited patiently and resignedly all this time: she was obviously used to this sort of thing. Finally we were off in a chartered taxi, very uncomfortable, smelly and dirty, after Mr Everly had made it quite clear that we were not going to pay anything extra for this trip. (The price was in fact included in the official Intourist ticket covering our hotel expenses in Khabarovsk.)

The first thing the lady guide pointed out to us was the hospital, right next to our hotel. The local hospital is always one of the first things guides point out to tourists. The only other edifice I can remember being shown was the Russian Railway High School, a most uninteresting structure which our guide seemed to regard as a kind of cathedral of technology. We were shown no churches: I was hoping to find one on my unguided strolls round the town, but had no luck. The guide told us that Khabarovsk had a sister-city affiliation with the Japanese town of Niigata, on the Japan Sea coast just across the sea from Khabarovsk.

Then we drove round the amusingly named 'Virgin Lands'—the outskirts of the town on which hundreds of blocks of workers' apartments, all identical, had risen. It was all featurelessly boring, and even the everlasting, quick-growing aspens that had been planted everywhere had a repetitious look. 'Neither use nor ornament,' as my mother would have said.

The lady told us she was a teacher of Russian literature. Chekhov was her passion, Vladimir Nabokov her *bête noire*: 'Ah yes, we have heard of *him*, he is a typical example of decadent capitalist art, but we never read him, he has no interest for me.' The hippie asked about 'free verse'. It does exist, and the Russians call it, she said, 'white verse', presumably because it leaves so much white paper on the sparsely printed page. She told us there were several poets in Khabarovsk, but they had been forced to turn to the writing of novels about good Russian workers. Mr Everly surprised me by saying he had written a graduation thesis on Dostoevsky; he asked her what she thought of this writer. 'Ah, he is what we call a "sick" writer, like Gogol,' she replied authoritatively and changed the subject. It was obviously the official line on Dostoevsky. When Everly asked her if she had heard of Nabokov's *Invitation to a Beheading* she simply shook her head and put on dark glasses.

We asked her about culture in Khabarovsk. There were several cinemas—later she came back to my hotel to tell me the exact number, which is fifty—with prices ranging from twenty-five to forty kopeks. There were two theatres and a music-hall. Foreign films were shown: English movies and 'frank' Italian ones, especially those satirizing

American and capitalist life, were much appreciated, but not Westerns or biblical epics, gangster thrillers and 'sexfilms' as she called them, 'which corrupt the purity of the young'—a common Western fallacy too. It is life itself that is the corrupter.

There is a speed limit, she suddenly informed us, of forty k.p.h., although traffic is almost non-existent. She gave us her opinions on sport: 'Football is not suitable for women, but for men it is a noble sport. I like swimming in summer. I detest "catch" [pro or all-in wrestling], it is so inhuman and beastly. I am very surprised Japanese people like such a "non-culture" sport so much.' This last view echoes my own.

Shrubs and flowers overflowed some of the dingy apartment balconies, whose outer rail was a sheet of corrugated iron painted in some primary colour that had long since faded and become covered with rust. A balcony to every flat seems to be the standard fixture in all modern blocks. All windows are double-glazed against the searing Siberian cold. But plumbing still seems to be inadequate. Though a magnificent ornamental fountain was playing among the flower beds in Lenin Square, only a few paces away, in the shadow of my hotel, there were lowly houses whose inhabitants were carrying buckets of water from communal stand-pipes. In the older 'Chinese' sector of the town—one cannot really call the place a 'city'—there are still some picturesque brick houses with decorated windows and shutters. These old houses also have double windows, filled with cottage garden flowers, geraniums, ferns.

Our guide gave us one example of Russian humour, the kind of grim humour we find in a story like Gogol's *On the Steppes*. She said: 'Khabarovsk is in three parts. Old Khabarovsk, New Khabarovsk (on the other bank of the Amur) and the third part is the cemetery.'

We got to Stadium Park, an old-fashioned pleasure garden laid out attractively and spaciously along the bank of the great River Amur. In parts, with its cement balustrades and steps and flower beds and shrubberies, it reminded me of the old North Marine Park in South Shields. But it also contained a modern football stadium and a large swimming-pool, both with sham Grecian façades and lifeless statues of athletes, the males always in form-suppressing slips, the females always in non-revealing tights or garments of some kind. There was no exposure of an entirely naked form anywhere to be seen. Prudery, prudence or prurience?

By the water under the long, concrete embankment were hundreds of Sunday fishermen fishing for carp, and scores of bathers. We walked on to a hillock at the end of the esplanade, on which stood a sort of Greek temple from which we could look down upon a long, curved beach thick with humanity. 'Like a carpet', our guide suggested. The people below looked like seething confetti.

Across the Amur I had clear views of a range of dark mountains— the border dividing Russia and Mongolia. Later I discovered that there was a telescope down on the beach by a coastguard house: I asked if I might use it (I was then alone, and easily recognizable by my clothes as a foreigner), but although some small boys had been playing around with the telescope just before, permission to look through it was refused me.

We moved on uphill to the other exit to the park, where our taxi had been instructed to wait for us. I should mention here that my hippie companion had drawn looks ranging from incredulity to open merriment, but there had never been any hostility. I had just taken some pictures of the town band playing near the park gates—the trumpeters were so convulsed with mirth at the sight of the hippie and myself that they blew a number of false notes, and the trombone player gave what sounded very much like a luscious raspberry on his instrument. I turned round to my companions just in time to see a middle-aged peasant attacking my hippie, while the lady guide, adjusting her dark glasses, moved on smoothly but swiftly to the gates, beckoning us to follow her. But the peasant had seized the hippie by the chignon and seemed about to strike him with clenched fist. Fortunately this large countryman, who wore a look of absolutely scandalized horror, had a giant of a wife, very brawny in her flowered frock, who restrained him by shouting what were obviously strong words and dragged him bodily away.

The lady guide, shaking all over, was anxious to get us away from the scene of the awkward *contretemps* and kept beckoning us towards the taxi. As I was more or less respectably dressed, in dove-grey pants, a Filipino *barong tagalog* (the first ever seen in Khabarovsk, I feel pretty sure), jewelled Japanese sandals and a number of Chinese jade rings, I attracted much less attention than my hippie comrade. We both stayed outwardly calm, though as I went to stand close beside him, to show my solidarity with him, I could see he was very pale and shaken by this very uncultured attack on him by an ignorant peasant.

With infinite leisureliness, I walked with the hippie towards the gate, where we turned our backs boldly upon the sniggering provincial ignoramuses of Siberia. Though I thought the hippie was really both crude and immature, at such a moment I would have demonstrated my solidarity with him against the whole of Russia. We escaped unhurt.

3
ON MY OWN IN KHABAROVSK

I HAVE been in Siberia only two days. On my first visit to a foreign land I do not usually try to sum up the character of the inhabitants after such a short acquaintance. However, I sometimes jot down my first impressions, for I have found that first impressions, though they may err in some respects, contain, on later consideration, germs of truth. Indeed, at the end of my second journey through Siberia about three months later, I looked again at my early notes about the appearance and personality of the Russians, and found my opinions had not changed at all.

The only Russian I ever knew personally in England was the painter Jacob Kramer, a wonderful man and an exuberant personality, full of mischief and snide Jewish humour, who was the only real friend I had during the two ghastly years I spent as Gregory Fellow in Poetry at Leeds University. Poor Jacob is now dead. Perhaps I was hoping to meet his like in Russia, but I never did. Only when I reached Poland did I see a few leonine, saturnine heads and massive, shambling bodies and wry smiles changing suddenly to wild laughter that reminded me of Jacob. The Epstein bust of him as a young man, in the Tate Gallery, was another image I carried in my mind throughout Russia. But I never saw anything like that massive sensitivity and lean intensity and wild defiance among Russian men. Jacob Kramer was a type of Russian that seems to be now extinct.

My first impressions of Russians, at Nakhodka and Khabarovsk, was that they were very large, raw, brutish, unsmiling, brooding, melancholy, sad, dour, silent. 'Great hulking brutes' was a pat phrase, but one which did indeed describe them accurately. Yet often those great heads and tremendous shoulders had the monumental weight and motionless force of a dynamo.

Nearly every working-class man looked like a 'hero of Soviet industry'—an unwilling hero, for one of the characteristics of modern Soviet man is that he does the absolute minimum of work required of him. This is as one would expect in a civilization geared to relieving the workers' lot. After all, work is an unpleasant necessity, and if one can get away with doing nothing one should do so. 'Heroes of industry' are few in comparison with the millions upon millions of worker drones.

But many of those men and women were impressive in their solidity and four-squareness that appeared to contain ominous reserves of power, violence, anguish, fear. Never once a smiling face: in Siberia, at least, smiles must be regarded as a form of weakness. Those who do not know them often say the Japanese and the Chinese are 'inscrutable', with 'faces like masks'. Though I do not really know them, I might equally well say the same thing of the Russians I have seen. They betray nothing, as if the display of human emotion might lead them into a trap. And there was in any case little motility in those strong necks, rigid jaws, thick, level, blond brows, downturned mouths of both men and women. The men in their shirt-sleeves—always cheap, old-fashioned rayon shirts with shapeless collars—had enormous forearms, thick wrists and fingers shaggy with bright yellow or ginger hair: thickets of brown or blond hair appeared above the top white button of their open-necked rayon shirts. The women's huge legs, statuesque as Picasso's neo-Grecian dream-women's limbs, were also bare, covered with fair down. Both sexes tramped purposefully along in what was almost the regulation footwear for summer: heavy, openwork sandals with sling backs, of antiquated design and quite without style.

Many of the younger men reminded me with hopeless nostalgia of my boyhood heroes on Tyneside—the miners, seamen, shipyard workers and their big, thick-thewed, football-playing sons, working-class lads, canny fellers, flowers of the factories, yards and pits. But the Russians had none of their gaiety, wildness and grace, their sudden shouts and flashing smiles in coal-dusted faces, their carefree whistlings and songs.

There was nothing volatile about the Russians in Siberia, which perhaps accounts for my sense of the great contrast between them and the Japanese. Instead, under their shapeless suits and dresses, constructed as if out of metal, I divined massive, muscular forms moving with measured tread, forms which made heroic official Soviet sculpture and propaganda posters not so improbable after all. Those tall idealizations of Soviet youth whose grubby, faded colours still startlingly adorn the blank-walled rectangular ends of Nakhodka's dreary blocks of workers' flats are not so far removed from actuality: I saw everywhere in Siberia those gigantic forearms, those broad, full throats whose noble tendons were tensed by the turn of questing heads and narrowed eyes of pioneers. Those bodies and faces were unforgettable in their strength, hardness and rigid determination. They are indeed like beings from another world.

We were whisked quickly back to the hotel by our lady interpreter and guide, who saw us into the lobby with evident relief. To my surprise, quite a crowd of young Russian hippies had gathered to welcome their American brother: somehow the word had got round that he was in town, and these young men began collecting round him. I knew they were hippies because their clothes were freer and more individual than those of the ordinary run of Russians. Their hair was not dressed in the usual spiv-like style for men, the straight crop or frizzy perm or old-fashioned bleached beehive for women. They nearly all wore dark glasses and displayed some small item like an American college fraternity ring (imitation) or sweat-shirts or socks or shoes which were obviously not Russian. I was to see more of them later.

I went straight up to my room for a shower. The heat of Siberia is intense in summer, though not as humid as in Japan or Korea. In the restaurant, after a long, long wait, I finally succeeded in attracting the attention of a tall, very snooty waitress—nowhere else in the world have I seen such a combination of grimness and prettiness on a woman's face—and after another long wait managed to extract from her a bottle of fairly cold dry champagne. One can tell it is dry because it has CYXOE printed on the black, white and gold label.

On the enormous menu nearly everything was 'off'. I finally selected a 'mixed cold meat dish'. It was perfect, with a scraping of red radish, a few fingers of shallot greens, two slices of cooked cucumber, several wafers of salami, three small chunks of beef, part of the spine of (apparently) a hare: it looked quite attractive except for one other item—a huge, neatly folded slice of pure white pork fat, which I at first took to be fish and conveyed to my mouth before realizing its awfulness. It took some time for this dish to arrive, and I sat sipping my champagne—rather tasteless and much too gassy—observing my surroundings and fellow diners. The dining-room was plain and undistinguished except for its extremely high ceilings. There was a small dance floor and a platform for a dance band, but there was no activity in those areas. I suppose the Central Hotel in Khabarovsk, like the innumerable, identical Centralhotellets in provincial Swedish towns (which indeed it much resembled) represents *le high life* of Khabarovsk. For Sunday dinner every man was in his shirt-sleeves, rolled up above the elbow, as if for serious work, open-necked—not a tie or a jacket to be seen apart from mine. Women were in dull, flowered cotton summer frocks. Eventually a man looking for a table in the crowded room came and sat beside me, asking me in Russian if the seat was free. He had obviously taken me for a Russian, as many Russians did, though most had spiv-like hairdos, sideburns, sometimes pompadours; women had tight perms.

It took ages to get service, ages to get wine and food and ages to get my bill. Finally, I just got up and walked out without paying. The waitress came running after me into the lobby, a cross expression on her face: I gave her my tiresome bundle of meal tickets and she selected one or two, then I had to pay something extra in cash. No tip. (But they're not averse to palming a little gratuity or a gift from abroad: this seems to grease the works a little and slightly speeds up service, elicits a faint amiability.)

After my conducted tour I set off to take an unofficial walk round Khabarovsk, all on my own. I was hoping to find where the gilded youth of the town congregated. The lady from Intourist had in fact shown me everything, but nothing I really wanted to see. It was better to go unaccompanied, as I always do in a foreign land whenever possible. I was not followed, at least not by anyone attractive, and I just went wherever the fancy took me. Owing to the fact that most Siberian Russians are of Latvian origin, I with my Scandinavian-Baltic-Viking air excited no comment as long as I wore subdued clothes. After Japan, where I am constantly stared at because I look so exotic and different from the Japanese, it was a curious feeling to walk the streets of Khabarovsk unnoticed.

But I had forgotten my expensive and elegant Italian shoes. Soon these began to receive longing and admiring glances from both men and women: they were so utterly un-Russian. Despite the general dowdy appearance of the Russians, they have a passionate interest in fine things, especially clothes and accessories. The next day too my sharp lemon yellow Chelsea boots of supple suède caused much nudging and comment among the men.

Though it was a Sunday and a holiday (I was surprised to find that

Sunday was a holiday in godless Russia!) most people were not strolling leisurely, but striding along in a very purposeful manner, as if proceeding according to orders from point to point, carrying bags and shopping-nets. They all seemed to have definite aims in mind. And how the booted, baggy-pantalooned soldiers marched along! There was none of the haphazard strolling of the Japanese, who wander dreamily all over the pavements, rambling erratically from one side to the other, as Coleridge is said to have done when he was out walking.

On Lenin Square there were scenes of great bourgeois domestic contentment: couples courting, marrieds with kids hiring for their offspring small pedal-cars which the youngsters drove sedately round and round one particular flower bed and no farther. No child ever dreamed of pedalling his car away from the stipulated route. The fond parents queued patiently and docilely, in perfect order, to rent these toy cars for five minutes at a time, and small tricycles too. It was probably the nearest most of those small children would ever come to owning a car. The streets were almost empty of vehicles and people therefore were able to cross the roads freely at any point. There are indeed sets of traffic lights at intersections, but no one takes any notice of them, for they are quite unnecessary: there is little traffic control, even on this holiday evening.

There were queues everywhere—for buses (packed and small and ancient), for ice-cream, for fizzy fruit drinks, for glasses of *kvass* drawn from cream-painted tanks standing at the side of the square. (Khabarovsk water is wellnigh undrinkable: it smells horribly of sulphur and rotten eggs and is a peculiar dark yellow colour, like animal urine. Drunk to excess, it causes stomach upsets and diarrhoea and nausea. Even the ice is yellow-brown. The poor Japanese business men stationed in Khabarovsk for the Trade Fair (a great success for Japan) were naturally distressed by this wretched water, for the Japanese reverence the purity of the crystal stream. Often the water in my hotel bathroom was a muddy brownish-black. One night when I was unbearably thirsty—there was no bar, and the restaurant closed at 11 p.m.—I drank two glasses of this stale, brownish-yellow water that had obviously been standing for days in a grimy pitcher on my dressing-table. I took the precaution of dissolving two *Cebion* tablets in it, and fortunately suffered no ill effects. It is therefore quite understandable that fruit juice and *kvass* are popular in summer in Khabarovsk, as they are indeed in all Russian towns.

I took some pictures of the square and of the children, who were enchanting. I was just going to walk down Lenin Avenue when I was approached by a youth of eighteen or so and three companions. They introduced themselves, speaking broken English; or rather their leader introduced them to me, mentioning each boy's name in turn. We all shook hands. The leader, whose name was Alexei, asked me my name and I said 'Hammond Innes', which he wrote down in a little notebook, using the Cyrillic alphabet.

'What you think Khabarovsk?' asked Alexei, the spokesman, for the other three who never uttered a word, at least not in English; even their Russian was scant.

Of course I replied that it seemed a very nice place and they all seemed very pleased. Then Alexei commanded me to follow him: it was a definite command; he wanted to show me the town, he declared. It never entered his head that I might already have been shown the the town. But this is always the typical experience of the foreign tourist: one is always assumed, by the natives, to have seen nothing and to know nothing, though it is common knowledge that excellent guide-books on almost every country in the world do exist.

We all set off down Lenin Avenue, he pointed out the obvious all the way: 'That is department store.'

Its drab, half-empty windows, with symmetrical pyramids of one unappetizing-looking tinned food, reminded me of the Co-op in war time.

'That is tobacco kiosk. That is cinema show frank Italian film Sophia Loren [*Marriage Italian Style*].'

Siberians are avid movie-goers. Recent data tells us that the average citizen (which means practically everybody) in the Kamchatka Peninsula visits the cinema forty-one times a year. In an article from Tass News Agency we learn that helicopters are frequently used in the delivery of films to remote fishermen's settlements and isolated communities in the Taiga. In Khabarvosk over two hundred new Soviet and foreign films are exhibited in a year. Japanese movies are popular in Asiatic Russia—*Red Beard, The Genius of Judo* and Ichikawa's splendid documentary on the Tokyo Olympics have all been great successes. The number of cinemas is growing all the time, and in Khabarovsk alone eleven big wide-screen cinemas are now being built.

The cinema we were passing looked small and scruffy: there was a seemingly endless queue waiting to get in. I was about to take a picture of this scene when Alexei stopped me, saying:

'Please do not take photograph, it is not good scene. That is Far Eastern Hotel.'

Outside the hotel I asked the boys to pose for a picture. At once they looked confused and unwilling, and one even turned his face to the wall. Alexei asked me not to photograph them saying:

'We have not good clothings and bad shoes.'

I thought it was very odd, for the boys were dressed no better and no worse than the other citizens of Khabarovsk, some of whom, I noticed, were covertly casting suspicious glances at the company I was keeping. I began to feel somewhat uneasy. Were these teenagers schoolboy gangsters?

We walked on down Lenin Avenue towards the Park of Culture and Rest. Just before entering Khabarovsk's other big open space, Komsomol Square, with its Red Star-topped obelisk and heroic statuary at the centre, Alexei suddenly asked:

'What do you collect?'

I racked my brains but could think of nothing but 'Varieties of sexual experience', which he would not have understood. However, my inability to answer him did not matter: all he wanted was to tell me what *he* collected. This tortuous method of giving information is in fact very oriental. Out he came with it:

'I collect ball pens, cigarette lighters and foreign marks,' he stated, looking at me to see if I showed any reaction. By 'marks' I presume he meant postage stamps.

'Oh, really?' I politely murmured. The childish talk and the youths' oppressive company were boring me. And I sensed what the next question was going to be:

'Have you any souvenirs?' Alexei abruptly inquired.

'No,' I answered, my heart sinking. But I thought it just possible he might mean souvenirs of Khabarovsk. At that moment one of the other boys offered me a Russian cigarette, which I accepted with an inward groan. It was one of the kind called *papyrosi* with only about two inches of loosely packed tobacco dust at the end of a four-inch cardboard tube. I had tried one before and found it appalling. They showed me how to pinch the cardboard mouthpiece, first horizontally then vertically, to prevent the little bits of dry tobacco dust entering one's mouth. Then we all stopped as I fished in my shoulder-bag for my Japanese cigarette lighter, a pretty Bronica of very modern design, one of the going-away presents given me before I left Japan. As it had been given to me by my friend and translator Shozo Tokunaga it was a treasured possession.

At once Alexei was all excitement. 'Give me cigarette lighter!' he cried. 'I want cigarette lighter for souvenir of you.'

I explained that it was a present from a close friend in Japan and therefore could not be parted with. Alexei nodded impatiently, then went on:

'Give me your souvenir. Give me ball-point pen. Give me foreign cigarette. Give me chewing-gum.'

'I do not use chewing-gum,' I replied. 'I am not an American.'

'You not give me souvenirs?' he asked with angry incredulity. 'We schoolboys, now holiday, we wish peace and friendship with foreigners. So give me your souvenirs. Give me peace souvenirs.'

'Goodbye,' I said as we entered the Park of Culture and Rest. I turned away from him quite impolitely, without shaking his hand. The boys walked away rapidly in the opposite direction, for the park attendant in his bemedalled white military-style jacket had appeared in the distance. I breathed a sigh of relief.

That was the sort of experience I was to have many times in Khabarovsk and in other Russian cities. Indeed the very next day I met Alexei in the park again and he started the same game, but adopting a different technique. He thrust upon me a cheap Mitsubishi ball pen, the sort given away free in Japan. I refused to take it as I knew he would ask for something in return. Even though I did not accept his 'peace souvenir' he followed me quite shamelessly, pestering me for 'ball pen, chewing-gum, cigarette lighter', and attracting the curiosity of passers-by, none of whom stopped to reprimand him for his bad behaviour.

Finally I got rid of him by jumping into one of the rare little grey taxis that by great good fortune happened to be cruising by just then. He ran to the door of the cab, pulled an exceedingly dirty comb in a cheap plastic sheath marked MOCKBA and thrust it through the window at me.

'Souvenir of me!' he shouted, grinning. I accepted it and waved him a smiling farewell. In the end I felt rather sorry for him: he had done very badly out of me. I learnt from the Japanese at my hotel that the Russians were mad about ball pens because these are not made in the Soviet Union, and the supply from Red Chinese factories had stopped.

4
THE RUSSIAN SHRUG

ONE strange feature of the streets in Khabarovsk was the total absence of dogs and cats. I suppose pets are considered to be unproductive and uneconomical in the daily struggle for existence.

I went into one or two of the *gastronom* (grocer shops) and department stores. Everywhere there was a very shoddy, poor selection of goods, and many empty shelves. Again I had the impression of that meanness and parsimony which characterized Britain during and after the Second World War. In one *gastronom* I bought a small cake of very inferior soap. I could find no after-shave talcum, which I had forgotten to bring with me from Tokyo, and none of the newer toilet requisites now considered necessary to the well-groomed comfort of modern man. Female make-up was in short supply and very expensive, and of course there were no male perfumes and cosmetics: these must seem terribly decadent to the Russians.

The women assistants in the stores were all, without exception, sour-faced, glassy-eyed, utterly unhelpful. There were long queues in the stores too. Then in the Far Eastern Hotel buffet-cum-grocer's, where I had a bite of breakfast one morning, there was another queue at the counter for brown bread, butter, cheese, meat (tough, dry, overcooked), pork fat, sour cream and black coffee. My thick chunks of bread, the butter and the cheese and meat were all placed on a plate and carefully weighed by the bad-tempered serving-woman, who was a mountain of fat.

Nowhere but in Russia have I seen so many hideously fat women. They seem to be quite satisifed to be overweight: perhaps they feel all that fat is a good investment, a standby for a possible rainy day or a buffer against the Siberian snow and ice. Certainly these fat women are completely unself-conscious about showing off their revolting cushions and rolls of flesh, for they wear bright, flowered cotton, tight-fitting frocks, and on the very dirty beach along the Amur at Khabarovsk they paraded by the scores wearing nothing but exiguous bikinis—one of the most repulsive human sights I have ever witnessed. Elderly men and crippled war veterans also think nothing of displaying their corpulence and infirmities to the public on the dance floor and at public bathing places. Young Soviet girls seem to think it a patriotic duty to invite mutilated ex-soldiers to fox-trot with them on the dance floors of hotels. I can see that there is something very laudable in this attempt to give pleasure and a taste of normal life to cripples who were probably heroes in the war against Fascism. But neither the men nor the girls really seem to enjoy it, and for spectators and other dancers the sight is one of painful grotesqueness. Only in Germany have I seen similar exhibitions.

One morning I walked into the little theatre on Lenin Avenue. It is quite lacking in charm or architectural distinction. Some stage hands were hanging green curtains to form wings: the dark, stuffy auditorium reminded me of those horrible drama boxes supported by the local bourgeoisie in small French provincial towns. I wish I could have seen a play performed there, but the season appeared to be over. In the foyer there were photographs of a recent production of a children's play—very bulky actresses dressed as butterflies and spiders and an actor in a sort of Mephistophelian spider outfit—a Russian Batman? All the costumes looked tatty and badly made. The play seemed to have been a mixture of *Peter Pan, Noddy in Toyland* and *Where the Rainbow Ends*.

Twice I went for a walk in Khabarovsk's other public park, the one surrounding the Dynamo Football Stadium, just behind Lenin Square. My first visit was at night, when it soon became obvious that this place, left more or less unlighted, was the centre of Khabarovsk's illicit amours. The second visit was on a sunny afternoon when I was rewarded by the sight of splendid girl athletes from a neighbouring high school in training: they were most extraordinarily beautiful creatures, strong and graceful and happy: they had still not been dulled and thickened and disappointed by life.

However, on both occasions I was severely bitten by voracious mosquitoes. Mosquitoes in Siberia! I thought they had all been wiped out by a rigorous extermination programme. It is said that the greatest hardship that had to be suffered by pioneers opening up the virgin lands of Siberia was the dreadful menace of these avid mosquitoes. The workers on the magnificent new dam at Bratsk—a truly monumental achievement—were bothered not so much by the perishing cold of central Siberia as by the pitiless swarms of mosquitoes and gnats that made their lives a misery. A rigorous programme of extermination was set in motion, and eventually the tundra and the taiga were cleared of these obnoxious pests.

But there are obviously still some pockets of resistance, and one of them is the Dynamo Stadium in Khabarovsk. It must be very uncomfortable for the earnest courting couples one sees there, immersed in their five-year plans for a happy future. The bites I received left me in agony for nearly a week. However, this was the one place in Khabarovsk where I was pestered only by mosquitoes. They are said to be particularly bad this year round Lake Baikal, and the rivers Angara and Yenisei, which I shall be passing on the Trans-Siberian Railway. How the workers on that epoch-making railway must have suffered! But in those days there were no extermination programmes. They just had to put up with the discomfort and the agonizing itch.

The restaurant at the Central Hotel is supposed to open at 11 a.m., but when I arrived for lunch just after noon the doors were still locked, and outside stood an angry queue. Despite constant banging and shouting from hungry comrades, the waitresses, who could be seen moving about inside, leisurely setting the tables, refused to open. I sensed they were enjoying a revengeful triumph over the customers, exerting what little power they possessed. These waitresses were among the most unpleasant I have ever met. The cult of personality is supposed to have been wiped out in Russia: I would recommend the authorities to take a good look at these waitresses and waiters in restaurants all over the Soviet Union, who keep asserting their individuality and trying to demonstrate their superiority in a most un-Soviet way. They are secret capitalists too, for they never turn down a tip, as every Japanese waiter and waitress is trained to do. I was beginning to feel, by now, very nostalgic for ordinary Japanese courtesy, smiling friendliness and willingness to give service. It is possible to give attentive service to others without feeling or appearing inferior: those Russian waiters and waitresses all seemed to resent serving their fellow men, as if they were afraid of losing caste or class. So they took it out on the customers by asserting their individuality and independence: there is nothing wrong with these qualities, but they should not be used as weapons to intimidate and humiliate one's fellow men. I shall never forget the sight of respectable, patient, well-behaved Japanese business men, professors, students and tourists quietly but thoughtfully accepting the bad service and the insults that are daily meted out in hotels, restaurants and Intourist offices.

I was constantly coming across scenes of bad temper and public quarrelling, something one almost never sees in Japan, where the provocations to lose one's self-composure are surely the most extreme in all the world. I took the small, packed, slow-moving bus from Komsomol Square up Lenin Avenue to Lenin Square, and all the way was witness to a bitter exchange of insults, fist-wavings, shrugs and contemptuous glances filled with dire hatred between the squat conductress, cosily ensconced behind her tickets in a seat near the door, and two female passengers defiantly waving their small white paper tickets. I gathered that the conductress was accusing them of travelling with used tickets. The two females were standing near the other door at the front of the bus. Their most interesting weapon in their armoury of gestures was the shrug, that shrug I was to see so often in Russia during displays of bad temper. It is not like the French or Italian shrug, half humorous, half despairing. It is not like the fatalistic Arab shrug or the resigned shrug that sometimes accompanies the Japanese sigh of 'Shikataganai'—'It can't be helped. . . .' The Russian shrug is a weapon in the battle for existence. It very definitely is an insult, expressing contempt, spite and loathing, and indicates venomous hatred for the person towards whom it is addressed. That shrug is the expression of the modern Russian soul—resentful, frustrated, bad-tempered, ever on the defensive, ever imagining slights, ever self-centred. It has no gaiety, no carefree Latin irony, no philosophical oriental passivity, no charm, no wit. It is the one gesture a Russian can make against authority: no wonder it is bitter.

Nevertheless in Khabarovsk I encountered two examples of Russian kindness, two of the occasions during my trips through Russia when I was treated with anything like human warmth. Both occasions were connected with machines. In Lenin Avenue there is a row of bright red machines dispensing soft fruit drinks of a revolting insipidity. I wanted to try one, but I was still not familiar with the coinage and did not know what coin to put in the slot. A pretty young girl, brown-skinned, dark-eyed, hair bleached white by the Siberian sun, came along and inserted two of her own coins for me and operated the buttons. She handed me the paper cup with a lovely smile, and at once my heart went out to her, she was so young, so pretty and so unspoilt by life; she was about eighteen, but still with the fresh heart of a child. She then got a drink for herself and we silently, smilingly, toasted one another with that dreadful synthetic juice. She would not allow me to repay her. I wondered if she was expecting a 'souvenir' in return, but no. Instead she took me to an art dealer's shop which was also Khabarovsk's biggest book store on a corner of Lenin Square near the Central Hotel. In halting German she told me she was studying painting, and pointed proudly to some awful reproductions of official Soviet portraits in the shop. There were other prints a little more modern in style, slick semi-abstractions, water-colour landscapes, innocuous domestic scenes. By accident, I discovered some books of satirical cartoons, and these, of an extreme frankness and cruel wit, raised my spirits considerably. They revealed to me that the Russians still possess a sense of humour, albeit a savage, inhuman one. These cartoons of family life in the vast new apartment blocks were unrelentingly anti-romantic, anti-domestic, anti-authoritarian. When the girl saw me smiling at them she whispered, looking cautiously round the shop to see if we were being observed: 'Nicht gut, nicht gut.' Then directed my attention to a plaster bust of Lenin which seemed to have been made from icing-sugar.

The second kind encounter was in the Central Hotel, not long before my departure for Moscow on the Trans-Siberian Railway. In the lobby there is a machine vending picture postcards and letter forms. I found I had no 5-kopek coin necessary to obtain a letter form. A middle-aged woman with the face of Grock the clown came up to me, took a 5-kopek piece from her purse and inserted it in the machine for me. She too refused to let me repay her. For one dreadful moment I thought she was going to ask to be repaid with a kiss. The coy way she put on one side her large, square, blank, masculine face with the small black eyes and roguishly pursed her lips gave me a nasty fright. Stammering thanks in broken Russian learnt from a phrase-book, I backed away to the safety of the Intourist desk.

Our Intourist guide who was to conduct us to the station that day was a slight young woman like a small brown flustered hen trying to collect all her chicks together. She looked hot and flushed with anxiety, and her brown, mousy hair was beginning to straggle over her cheeks in a way I always find infinitely touching in a woman.

Though I had booked (and paid for) travel in 'soft class' for the return journey on the Trans-Siberian Railway, I was to be in 'hard class' for the whole of the six days' journey from Khabarovsk to Moscow. And J.T.B. in Tokyo had apparently not paid the required reservation fee, so I had to deplete my small store of cash by paying out an extra two roubles.

When we got to the station the hippie's reservation fee was also discovered not to have been paid. At once he refused to pay it, declaring roundly: 'Let them deport me! I'm not paying anything!' I meekly paid my two roubles, secretly admiring the hippie's stand. She privately told me that in order to avoid embarrassment for herself and the hippie she had paid his reservation fee out of her own pocket. (Two roubles is about thirteen shillings, quite a large sum of money for a poorly paid Intourist guide.)

But even worse was to happen. The poor girl discovered at the last moment that there were no seats for eight of the foreigners who had been with me all the way from Yokohama! There was a great outcry at this. Fortunately my own berth was assured. The guide, flushed with terror, her brown hair in ever more distraught wisps round her bird-like features, finally managed to locate four extra places, but the other four foreign passengers had to be left behind to spend yet another day and night in Khabarovsk. They were a Norwegian and his wife and two sons. The father, a Communist, had carefully trained his beard to make him look exactly like Lenin, a fact of which he was very proud, but upon which, curiously enough, no Russian ever remarked.

'Don't you think I look like Lenin!' he would keep asking astonished Russians, who would reply, politely but unconvincingly:

'Oh yes, yes, of course. Just like our great Lenin.'

I sensed that the Russians felt it was sacrilege for anyone to imitate Lenin.

My Intourist porter happened to be a hippie type with a mushroom cut and a faded American sweat shirt. He asked me what I thought about Russia. Just at that moment I was not feeling very gay so I snapped:

'Awful. England is much better.'

He flushed and said, angrily smiling:

'What about your seamen's strike?'

I, who felt full sympathy for our seamen's brave struggle for better working conditions, replied:

'At least *our* seamen are allowed to strike, and in the end will get better conditions. Your Russian seamen couldn't do that.'

'They don't need to and don't wish to strike,' he countered.

I felt this was probably quite true, for the Russians seemed to me a nation of sheep—angry sheep, but nevertheless sheep, and in sheep's clothing.

The hippie porter flung my suitcase on the platform from the back of his lorry, breaking a lock. No apology. He shouldered my bags and arranged them very inconveniently for me on the high shelf above my berth in the train. 'Have you any souvenirs?' was his final question. 'No.' He gave that depressing, disdainful, defensive Russian shrug. 'Good old England!' he said unexpectedly and quite without sarcasm. We waved a happy farewell. He was the only hippie at the station to see off his American brother-hippie. Perhaps the others had been warned. . . .

PART TWO

THE TRANS-SIBERIAN RAILWAY
Khabarovsk-Irkutsk-Moscow

I

ACROSS SIBERIA

AFTER all the confusions and recriminations, the diesel train of the Trans-Siberian Railway, coming from Vladivostok, set off from Khabarovsk station fairly promptly (just after 3 p.m., the official starting time) on Monday, 11th July 1966. I was in carriage No. 4, seat No. 21—an accommodation I was never to forget.

As we drew out of the station I saw the Norwegian 'Lenin' shaking his fists on the platform, his wife in a state of collapse, and the poor little Intourist woman now sobbing openly, vainly apologizing, her face white with terror.

'Soft class' simply means sharing a compartment with one other person instead of with three: but 'soft class', as I was later to discover on the train from Moscow to Leningrad, is also much more comfortable and cleaner than 'hard class'. I had been herded into a 'hard class' compartment, despite having paid through the nose for 'soft class' in the Tokyo J.T.B. office of Intourist, but I was so thankful even to get a seat on the train that I decided to make the best of things and keep my complaints for later. (I never did complain—I was too worn out when I got back to Tokyo—and I was never reimbursed by Intourist, which, once it gets its hands on dollars, does not like to give any of them back.)

I was in what surely must have been the most antiquated coach in the whole Russian railway system. There were white linen embroidered covers for the backs of the two lower bunks, but these were already grubby. There was one small table at the window on which stood a small lamp shaded with pleated pale green stuff: already dust lay thick in the sun-faded pleats. There was a wooden step-ladder for those unfortunates who had to sleep in the top bunks. Luckily I had a bottom bunk.

The compartment was infernally hot and stuffy, full of the stale air of the other travellers who had come from the terminus at Vladivostok. Fresh sheets, a pillow-case and a blanket were laid out for me by a cheerful train girl who spoke a little English. I tested my berth: fortunately I prefer a hard mattress as I have got so used to sleeping on the floor in Japan.

The window was thick with grime, the window-sills heaped with tiny cinders and dust. The handles on the steep steps to the carriages were coated with grease and grime, just like British Railways. The paint was peeling, the lavatories filthy. Nightly my pillow was snowed with soot, daily dredged with cinders, drifted with ash and sand. From time to time the corridors of the carriage were cleaned by the train girl or her elderly father with an antiquated vacuum cleaner. But they cleaned only the floor, not the window-ledges heaped with coal dust and grit or the table strewn with soot.

I think that like most people I had a romantic dream about the glamour of the Trans-Siberian Railway, of pink-shaded lights in dining-cars brilliant with ambassadors and beautiful spies, of dusky, scented compartments each of which contained a Madonna of the Sleeping Cars. I was prepared to give up all my secrets for a night of bliss—all for love, and the world well lost! I even had some fake documents which I had hoped to trade for forbidden kisses and perfumed, fur-swathed arms of mysterious, guttural-voiced beauties. Alas, how far was the reality from that schoolboy dream!

My compartment was shared with three men. Two of them seemed to be young labourers, who slept most of the time. The lower bunk opposite me was occupied by an old gentleman wearing steel-rimmed spectacles and a little embroidered skull-cap. He was always reading, and refused to speak to me until I asked the train girl to tell him I was not an American. At that, his charming old face beamed and he shook my hand heartily in both of his. It was the time of Wilson's visit to Moscow, and everyone was very keen on the British just then. The old man was a doctor of philosophy, and we chatted from time to time, in German, which he spoke fairly well, about Kant and Hegel and Husserl and Heidegger and of course Bertrand Russell, one of the great folk-heroes of Russian intellectuals. He said he was unable to read Wittgenstein, but whether he meant that this philosopher is too difficult or that he is forbidden in Soviet Russia I could not make out. I asked him about Russian philosophers, but he refused to talk, contenting himself only with a wry smile. Philosophy, after all, is hardly an aid to increased production. A few days later, when I fell ill on the train with a mysterious sickness, he gave me a tablet that cured me completely within a few hours. I began to look upon him as a magician, a kind of Russian Dr Coppelius, whom he indeed resembled.

In some of the compartments men and women were mixed. Some of the younger women had very decadent-looking Western-style dressing-gowns, but most of them were in the regulation flowered cotton dresses, or in track suits. Nearly all the men were wearing track suits, all of the same colour, dark blue. Some of the men had black alpaca pyjamas, and every Russian man I saw undressing on the train wore black alpaca underpants. All wore slippers or cheap sandals with those sling-back heels.

The train never travelled faster than about thirty miles an hour, and the carriages were so extravagantly sprung that one was continually bouncing about in a sickening way. This constant lurching made reading and writing very difficult and painful. The pages of my notebooks written on the train look like demented knitting.

There were fortunately no mosquitoes, but many flies, drunk with dregs of the weak, flat, bottled beer. No one dared to drink the water. Sometimes, apparently at the whim of the restaurant car manager, bottles of lemonade or mineral water were suddenly made available. Then the dining-car would be besieged with people clamouring for bottles of this disgusting pop. There were a few bottles of some quite good red wine from Georgia, the usual gassy Russian champagne and a kind of light, dry sherry and other wines from Tiflis and Samarkand. However, the stock of these soon ran out, except for the champagne.

The restaurant car menu, like all menus in Russia, was a farce. It was grandiose, as big as the Magna Carta, with a vast variety of dishes covering a score of pages. But of all these dishes only about six were available: these could be picked out because they had a price scribbled beside them in pencil. But even these marked dishes were often not available. Most of the passengers bought food at stations where the train would stop for five to fifteen minutes. In each carriage there was a list of train times, giving the exact number of minutes for each stop, and this time-table was adhered to rigidly.

As soon as the train came to a halt swarms of passengers, mostly in their track suits or underwear or pyjamas, would troop off and march in that purposeful Russian manner to a sort of long wooden shack by the railway lines in which would be standing a score or so of old women in the everlasting Russian headscarves, selling eggs, milk, sour cream, cucumbers, scallions, blueberries or strawberries or even cherries. Others had home-baked pies, pasties or cakes, all covered with flies. The passengers would descend upon these very individualistic and authoritarian old women like a swarm of locusts, and by the time the train left the counters would be cleared. Russians are for ever on the scrounge for food. The goods were not cheap either. A pint bottle of milk was thirty kopeks (about two shillings) and a twist of blueberries (most of them not quite ripe) twenty-five kopeks. It was daylight robbery, and an example of the much-denigrated private enterprise at its worst. Those capitalist peasant women selling produce at the wayside stations must have been making a fortune.

Where's the famous Russian samovar? The only samovar I'd seen so far was in a shop window in Khabarovsk. On the train there was a boiler in every carriage (but not a samovar). This water-heater was fed by sticks and charcoal by the old man and his daughter who were in charge of the carriage. Every morning about six they would begin stoking up, filling the carriage with choking, acrid smoke. It always took ages for the water to heat. Then they made black tea in a small teapot, very strong. This was poured, heavily diluted with boiling water, into glasses with metal holders, together with a packet of cement-like sugar (from Cuba) for each passenger. The brewing of the early morning tea was one of the nicest things in the day, one I always looked forward to. As the dawn broke over the tundra I would be sitting on a small, slippery strapontin by a window in the corridor, reading *Sodome et Gomorrhe* and waiting for the water to boil. They always brought me the first glass of tea, which I could replenish as many times as I liked. All through the day there was tea available. I thought it was free, but at the end of my journey I was asked to pay for all the glasses I had drunk: it was not very expensive. Dry, sweet wafer biscuits were also sometimes provided with the tea. There was never any other kind of biscuit.

From time to time a middle-aged, drunken 'soup boy' would pass down the corridors, carrying a wooden cradle filled with metal bowls of lukewarm, greasy beetroot soup. This was the famous *bortsch* (or *borsch* as it is sometimes spelt in English and German). It was very cheap, but not very appetizing. Another jovial old drunkard, like some character out of Gorky's *Lower Depths,* would sometimes stagger down the corridors selling chilled *compote*—a few stewed plums, apricots and cherries in a very weak suspension of fruit juice. It makes quite a delicious drink when cold, but should actually be avoided, as it tends to bring on colic, caused I think chiefly by the bad Russian water from which it is often made. The man dispensed his sludge in paper, or rather rough, thin, cardboard cups that dripped because the joins were so badly made at the bottom. When I bought a cupful the old man insisted on fishing up with his dirty fingers choice bits of plum and cherry to add to my already overflowing cup. I could not drink it. An old woman in a pinafore that had not been washed for weeks also came round selling things, chiefly sticky, fly-blown buns which I could not stomach but which the Russians wolfed down: they seemed to be forever eating something. No vodka or beer or lemonade was sold in the corridors: vodka was not allowed on the train.

Newspapers were in great demand at each station, though to my eye they looked abysmally dull. I noticed that the Russians just skimmed the headlines then threw the paper away or used them to make sun-hats or receptacles for the wild berries they purchased at such inflated prices from the station peasants. The only periodical they seemed to read with any pleasure or interest was the excellent satirical magazine *Krokodil*. Several people loaned me copies of this, and even I, who could read only a few words in Russian, found it vastly entertaining. (I had brought with me the M.I.T. Press's paperback edition of *The Learner's Russian-English Dictionary* by Lapidus and Shevtsova, which I can thoroughly recommend. I learnt quite a lot of Russian by studying *Krokodil* with the aid of this excellent dictionary.) In order to get a newspaper or magazine, one had to dash off the train and sprint along the platform to the book kiosk, where one had to push and shove wildly in order to get served. The Russians are no respecters of persons when it comes to buying two things— food and books. Then it's every man for himself, and no false chivalry in the treatment of women. These Amazons could hold their own with the biggest and strongest of men when it came to shoving their way to the front of a queue. There was a book and newspaper kiosk at practically every station, however small, and it was always besieged as soon as the train stopped. Russians are mad about books, but not, I think, in a strictly literary sense: they are mad about books as stamp-collectors are mad about stamps. Huge editions of approved Soviet and foreign authors (in Russian translation) appear on the market and these are immediately swept up by book collectors. Editions of hundreds of thousands can be sold out in a morning. Many of these editions are well-produced but are very cheap. It seemed to me that the Russians snapped these up because they are now conditioned to snap up anything on sale, no matter what it is: they are very commodity conscious and bargain conscious simply because there is no very great range of commodities. Buying up books is one aspect of the rapacious Russian character.

Translations are excellent. I found a copy of a quite interesting magazine, *Soviet Literature* published by the Union of Writers of the U.S.S.R., which contained a fascinating account of a symposium that had been held on the problems of literary translation. It was evident from this article that the Russians approach the task of translation with infinite care and with scientific sensitivity. The great Soviet authority on the theory of literary translation, Dr Andrei Fyodorov, is the head of a Literary Translation Studio which was originally founded in 1918 under the direction of Maxim Gorky and his World Literature Publishing House.

Many Russian translations of European literature have been so well done that they are thought of as original Russian works: Samuel Marshak's Burns, Tatiana Gnedich's Byron, Boris Pasternak's Goethe and Shakespeare. (Incidentally Pasternak was referred to with great respect as a translator at this symposium.) Recently there have been brilliant new translations like Nikolai Lyubinov's of Rabelais and Cervantes, Ivan Kashkeen's of Hemingway and Rita Right-Kovaleva's of Salinger and Faulkner. These translations are claimed by Fyodorov to be true works of art in their own right. As a professional translator, I felt great envy for the excellent conditions under which translators of literature work for the State. In Russia literary translation is rewarding in every way, for besides producing works of art the translators are highly paid, accorded great honours, and looked up to as literary geniuses in their own right. In England only two men, I think, have achieved such distinction—Arthur Waley and Scott-Moncrieff. It is not generally realized under what miserable conditions English translators work. We are rarely allowed to translate a book we *want* to translate, but instead we have flung at us some novel, autobiography or archeological work which a publisher has not read but just picked up, probably in a 'package deal', at some trade fair. Translation fees are wretchedly low, and the translator receives no royalty on sales of a book his talent may have turned into a best-seller. Therefore translators seldom have respect for the works they are asked to render into English: they just rush them off the typewriter as quickly as possible, and to hell with meaning or style. Britain and other countries would benefit a great deal, I am sure, from the setting up of Literary Translation Workshops on the outstanding Soviet pattern.

The old philosopher with whom I was travelling had a number of English and German books in translation—Dickens, Defoe, Carossa and *Till Eulenspiegel*, which he was constantly chuckling over. They were all cheap, but beautifully bound and printed, with excellent illustrations by Soviet artists. He was very impressed by my Pléiade edition of Proust and by a paperback of Charlie Chaplin's autobiography. Chaplin is reverenced in the U.S.S.R. both as a clown of genius and a victim of American persecution. I found that, simply by carrying this paperback book around, with the picture of Charlie as the immortal tramp on the cover, I could arouse the goodwill and friendly smiles of Russians everywhere. They were all looking forward to the Russian translation of this autobiography.

After the first day supplies on the train began to run low. There was no more beer, no lemonade, no mineral water. A few more of the marked items on the ambitious menu were 'off'. No salad, no vegetables, no milk. Only thick hunks of very salty brown bread, salty cheese and rancid butter. For breakfast on the first morning I was lucky to get a baked egg with a strip of synthetic ham. No bourgeois luxuries like toast, marmalade or coffee of course. But I did not mind because there was apparently still plenty of champagne and caviar. However, I wondered how long my money would last if I continued to live for the next five days on these somewhat expensive commodities. I had foolishly neglected to change a traveller's cheque in Khabarovsk. I only had about eight roubles with me, and a clutch of meal tickets. I found it was impossible to change money or travellers' cheques on the train or at the stations: I should have to wait until I got to Moscow.

The hippie from America never appeared in the dining-car. The elderly Swedish gentleman at whose table I had been sitting on the *Baikal* sometimes joined me for lunch or dinner and told me about the hippie, with whom he was sharing a compartment, to his great disgust. He complained of the hippie's smelly clothes and dirty feet and his habit of opening tins of food and drink at all hours of the day and night and scattering the discarded cans and packages all over the floor. The hippie's luggage was composed almost entirely of supplies of American canned foods. He also annoyed the very prim and proper Swede by reciting, or pretending to recite, Zen Buddhist sutras, sitting upright in the posture of Zen meditation, with crossed legs and joined hands in lap, right in the middle of the floor of the compartment.

I went along once or twice to say hallo to the hippie whom I could not help liking as long as I did not have to see too much of him or listen to too much of his pretentious literary and mystical chat. I found his compartment in a veritable state of chaos, with freshly washed socks hanging dripping from the ceiling light, and shirts and sweatshirts and jeans drip-drying over the windows. There was always a crowd of Russians round his door, gazing in spellbound at this fantastic, anarchic creature. But no one attacked him, and indeed he made one or two friends among the younger people. He was certainly an original, though his originality was in fact very conventional and stereotyped: one can find the same type by the thousand in San Francisco and New York.

Once I invited him to come and have dinner with me in the dining-car, but he refused, saying he did not like to be insulted by Russian waitresses, whom he referred to picturesquely as 'rancid udders'. Indeed they had often refused to serve him in Nakhodka and Khabarovsk. The two hard-worked waitresses in the dining-car, however, were the pleasantest and most good natured I was ever to meet in Russia. They were constantly on the go. One often had to wait a long time for service, but it was obvious that they were doing their best. As long as one waited quietly and patiently, and gave small tips and presents, they treated one fairly and efficiently and occasionally—oh, wonder of wonders!—rewarded one with a weary smile.

2

THE WORLD OUTSIDE

DAILY life in our compartment soon settled down into a communal routine—morning tea, queueing for the lavatory (filthy and stinking), breakfast, reading, writing notes, sleeping for an hour or so, reading, lunch, sleeping all afternoon, tea and biscuits, a sip from a private bottle of Stolichnaya vodka (marvellous), a chat, dinner, wine, more chat, reading, queueing for the lavatory, reading in bed, sleep.

The carriage in which my compartment was situated was a very ancient one, probably dating from the time of the building of the railway (by the French, who were never paid for it) in the 1880s. Massive ornamental woodwork, walls painted *caca d'oie*. Spotted mirrors. Cumbrous light fittings, heavy sliding doors. Imitation Turkey carpet on the floor and in the corridor, where it is protected by a green canvas runner. Greasy grime dusts and films everything, and my clothes are soon in a mess with oil and soot. But on the whole fairly bearable, despite the jolting. Lights are not switched on until it is really dusk. A constantly playing radio or tape of popular Red Army songs or folk-dances: there is a machine which relays these unwelcome accompaniments to my day at the end of every carriage, in a small room next to the one shared by the train girl and her old father, who are really immensely kind and nice, as are all the other people in the carriage. Living with them intimately, day by day like this, is a very good way to get to know the Russians, almost as good as living with them in one of their apartment blocks, something a foreigner would never be able to do, for the Russians fight shy of foreigners, mainly for security reasons, I think. They do not want to get involved with undesirables. But on this train we are all in the same boat: life is open, there are no secrets, nothing to hide, so that we live together on easy terms. I suppose that for most of the Russians on that train the trip was a kind of holiday; they were good tempered and friendly and out to enjoy themselves. They were delighted whenever I tried out my Russian phrases on them. Very few spoke English or any other language but Russian, but we managed to make ourselves understood by one another. For the first time in Russia, despite the discomfort, I felt happy.

Much of the gaiety and carefree atmosphere of our carriage stemmed from the presence in it of many members of the Bolshoi Circus, which I had attended with great delight in the Sendagaya National Gymnasium in Tokyo. Their Japanese tour over, they were travelling back to Moscow via Vladivostok and the Trans-Siberian Railway, though the stars of the show, including the delectable clown Popov, who were privileged People's Artists, had returned by the speedier and no doubt more comfortable Aeroflot service direct from Khabarovsk. (There is now a direct Tokyo–Moscow non-stop flight by giant TU-114 turbo-props that takes a route across Niigata and north of the Trans-Siberian Railway, passing over Magdagachi, Kirensk—from where Lake Baikal can be seen in the distance—and Sverdlovsk.)

At every stop the acrobats from the Bolshoi Circus would troop out on to the platform and do limbering-up exercises in their dark blue track suits, and perform miraculous balancing feats. Conjurers and jugglers sometimes amused us in the corridors as they practised their arts in the unsteady train. Accordionists and players of the balalaika would often serenade us, and the sound of Russians singing their madly melancholic or feverishly gay songs as the train lumbers slowly through the long sunsets over the tundra is something one never forgets. I remembered very well the enormously fat ringmaster I had admired for his poise and wit at Sendagaya: he was referred to by the rest of the troup very proudly as 'our entrepreneur'. The train girl said that one of the members of the troupe, which is always travelling abroad, might be able to cash one of my travellers' cheques for me, but later we discovered that this was not legal, so nothing came of it. The music, songs and laughter of the Bolshoi Circus were a great relief from the incessant canned music. Fortunately, in my compartment, the doctor of philosophy kept the music switched off: we soon came to an unspoken agreement on this point. The other two men were always sleeping. But when the train man used to come to vacuum our compartment every morning he would look up in surprise at the silent loudspeaker and turn it on full volume. After he had gone we would turn it off again. But strains of the everlasting marching and waltzing and folk-singing would penetrate from neighbouring compartments. The music always had that empty noise of music that no one is listening to. But the others never thought of switching off or turning down the volume. Sometimes when the occupants of the next compartment went for dinner I would creep in and turn down their volume: on their return from the dining-car, they noticed no difference. This nuisance was never switched off in the sound engineer's room until late at night, well after ten o'clock, when most people were already sleeping. There was no radio contact, apparently, with the outer world in those remote areas of Siberia between Khabarovsk and Irkutsk, for I never heard any news flashes until we were approaching Novosibirsk.

A small lunch: half a slice of thick brown bread and butter, a dish of fresh caviar—grey and gluey but exquisite—and half a bottle of well-chilled champagne. About twelve shillings, with a surreptitious tip to the waitress. With no newspapers and no wireless, I have no idea what is going on in the world, and it hardly seems to matter. We are travelling in a sort of timeless bubble. From the windows of dining-car and compartment I gaze and gaze in the utmost fascination at the world outside, a world that seems remote from all reality until we stop at a station and I can get out and make contact again with the earth.

At every station, even the smallest, there is a silver-painted mass-produced bust statue of Lenin. Sometimes a placard shows photographs of local 'heroes of production', both men and women, staring woodenly, with barely concealed, smug self-satisfaction, conscious of their worth. Sometimes there are other mass-produced statues, also painted silver, of footballers or idealized workers, ballerinas, children, cosmonauts.

The landscape: rolling green countryside patchworked with vast fields of hay or potatoes. An occasional lake, surrounded by the Russians' favourite tree, the silver birch, looking ethereally beautiful, ghostly, the summer leaves lightly shimmering in the breeze. Clusters of larch, aspen, acacia. The hayfields are brilliant with many-hued wild flowers: I had never dreamed that Siberia would look so lovely, so radiant with cornflowers, poppies, daisies, eglantine, honeysuckle, briar roses, meadowsweet, willowherb, great rafts of cow-parsley, trailing woodbine and morning glory and my favourite flower, the dandelion. The fields were starred with every colour of wild flower like a Swiss alp in May. It was a truly heavenly sight, and one I never tired of. At the end of the first day on the train there was an extremely long, late and glorious sunset over the vast, flat, lonely, empty horizon.

Everyone stood silently at the windows in the corridor of the slowly trundling train, gazing at the unearthly spectacle, whispering when the first weak star blinked out of the dusk in ever deeper darkness and silence. It was like being present at some forgotten religious rite. The silence was broken only by the switching on of the lights. Everyone sighed, moved, got ready for dinner. Beyond the windows the sunset and the world outside had suddenly vanished. We were back again within our timeless bubble, a pilgrim community, a freight of human souls brought together for a while by chance, and never to meet again.

There is no place like Siberia for giving man a sense of the triviality of his destiny, for giving him a correct perspective of himself in the universe, for reducing him to a scale of helpless, humiliating smallness —a brief, flickering shadow in the vast light of eternity.

3
ON TO OMSK

SECOND day, Tuesday, 12th July. I woke at seven in the morning. The time has been put back one hour. Between Khabarovsk and Moscow the time changes every day, but on the station platforms the clocks all tell Moscow time. This seems to me symbolic of the yearning of Chekhov's Masha, lost in the provinces, for far-off Moscow.

I had a comfortable night, but awoke with my hair and face covered with fine black dust and grit. It is impossible to wash my hair in the lavatory, where there is only cold water. The restaurant car does not open until ten o'clock, so the early morning glasses of tea, in which the sugar, the slabs of concrete, dissolved with infinite slowness, were very welcome. I slept most of the day, between doses of Proust and Charlie Chaplin. The countryside is still green and flowery, with only very occasional human beings, no houses between stations, no tractors, wagons or lorries in the fields. An occasional peasant scything hay, taking no notice of the passing train. No one waves to him, and even if one did he would not wave back. The inane jog-trot rhythm of the train wheels is very sleep-inducing. Though we are going so slowly the carriage still bounces about a great deal. A child is sick in the corridor, and I'm not surprised. It's worse than being at sea. Had some coffee for breakfast—a mistake, it was awful—and some bread, butter and slice of hard cheese.

Russia is planning to build a new Trans-Siberian Railway. It will cut the 4,000-mile journey from European Russia to the Pacific coast by 621 miles. The Soviet news agency Tass reports that it will take fifteen to twenty years to construct this new line, which will cross marshes, huge Siberian rivers and icy mountain ranges. I should have thought it would have been better, and cheaper, to improve the present rolling-stock and speed up the dismally slow trains.

Third day, Wednesday, 13th July. I awoke at dawn to find the train puttering along a wide misty river, which the professor says is the Shilka. Green misted mountains, osier-edged river banks, many small islands. On the opposite shore, a tall white steeple and the main building of what looks like a monastery. Soon, crossing a big, girdered bridge, we enter the station of ———. (How reminiscent this is of Russian novelists' curious suppressions of place-names in their works!) We stop here for a while. I dash out on to the platform and fight for some hard-boiled eggs and a bottle of milk plugged with a piece of dirty newspaper. People tussling for newspapers and books at the bookstall. Others making long queues for ice-cream.

The river is a magnificent sight, noble and broad like a river of Africa. Rivers are the veins and blood, the driving force and poetry of the Russian people. Everyone was at the windows to gaze in silent awe at this tremendous river. They gazed at that river as if it were a god, just as the Japanese gaze at a burning building. They began talking about it, discussing its good points as a farmer might talk of a favourite beast, as a sailor talks of the sea. At that moment I felt the soul of Russia breathing. 'Mother Russia.'

Noon: At Yuma, I went out on the platform, and nearly missed the train, which gives never a hoot to warn passengers it is leaving. I was staring at nothing in particular when I suddenly heard the train girl shouting, in the distance across the tracks:

'Englishman! You! Englishman!'

I turned round and saw the train beginning to glide away. I sprinted across the tracks and just managed to leap aboard, assisted by some of the circus acrobats. They swung me through the air and off the ground with the greatest of ease. I felt the phenomenal strength of their well-trained, muscular bodies. Two of the young men are obviously recently married. Their wives are young and pretty. They are obviously deeply in love and there is something deeply moving in their happiness together, in the sheer radiance that illuminates their faces and seems to shoot out rays of bliss from their bodies. I notice that the two couples, sharing a compartment, take it in turns to stand outside in the corridor while one of the couples remains inside, presumably making delicious, passionate love in the bumping, rocking train. How I envy them!

One of the young acrobats brought me some illustrated magazines, and proudly showed me pictures of Harold Wilson with Kosygin at the Moscow Conference. 'Peace!' cried the young acrobat, beaming all over his handsome face, that was deeply lined, with smouldering, sunken eyes. 'Peace! Peace! Peace!' he cried happily, like a child with a new toy, and wrung my hand in both of his enormous mitts, crushing my fingers with such force I thought he was going to fracture them. All Russians shake hands in this violently demonstrative way.

'Peace! Peace! Peace!' I cried in reply, smiling and laying my free hand on top of his. He seized me then in his arms and gave me a tremendous, bear-like hug, kissing me passionately on both cheeks, while everyone looked on, smiling indulgently and crying 'Peace!'

I was never at any time in any doubt about the Russian people's sincere desire for peace. They were always talking about it, and expressing their hatred of war, particularly of the loathsome conflict in Vietnam. They would become quite white with passion when discussing the horrors of this ghastly war, and spat out the names of Johnson, McNamara and Dean Rusk with the utmost contempt. That true desire for peace was the thing that I liked best about the Russians: they stuck to that ideal with such vehemence and single-mindedness. No other people express themselves so strongly about the need for peace except the Japanese. Their sincerity and utter honesty of mind in this matter are deeply impressive. They seize every opportunity they can find to impress upon foreigners this fundamental passion for peace and hatred of war. In this I found them truly admirable, and an example to the rest of the world's nations with their lukewarm shilly-shallyings about 'contained' wars, wars of defensive aggression and easily forgotten treaties against the spread of nuclear weapons and hydrogen bomb testings.

After making my bed I lay down again and looked out of the window at the simple beauty and grandeur of the landscapes: in such a beautiful land, so often devastated by wars, how could one not fervently long for peace?

I noticed, outside many small houses lost in the hay, a ladder leaning against the end wall, leading to the small, open wooden door of a loft, in whose dimness golden hay gleamed.

Fourth day, Thursday, 14th July. I have to put down the date every day, or I would soon, in this timeless bubble, lose track of the days. Today, new arrivals in our compartment, a mother and small boy. About midnight the man in the bunk above mine left the train, and another, who looks like a simple peasant, took his place. He made his own bed in the dark. It was difficult to sleep. I took a Nembutal and read Charlie Chaplin until two in the morning, when I fell asleep.

The doctor of philosophy woke me just before dawn for a view of the magnificent sunrise over Lake Baikal. Dizzy with Nembutal, I scrambled somehow into my clothes. The air was cool, the light was still dim, with a sliver of moon still visible. And there lay the beginning of the immense lake, immensely calm, deserted, lonely in the extreme, fringed by low mountains dark green with larch. A little farther on, as the light slowly increased, I saw two or three men fishing on the shore, a few horses grazing. They looked like animals at the beginning of Creation. Darkly silhouetted against the crimsoning lake, they appeared like a frieze painted by some primitive hunter in the depths of his cave.

As the lake became brighter it was reminiscent now and then of Lake Maggiore in its sheer size, stretching vast arms of water into the mountains. Here too were occasional little lakeside villages and profusions of wild flowers. Scarves of mist began to slowly rise and twist among the silver birches in the green lakeside meadows, where sparks of mica glittered wildly in sand and rocks. The lake went on and on. The train would leave the lakeside and run between mountains for a while. Just when I thought we had left the lake behind for good, it would suddenly appear again round a corner or at the end of a tunnel. We made a number of long stops at stations beside the lake. At one stop an adventurous young man, wearing only a jock-strap, dashed across the tracks and took a brisk bathe in the lake. He came back shivering in the hot sun, saying it was still icy cold!

All the passengers were at the windows, transfixed by the spectacle of this great stretch of water. I think it is worth getting off the train at Irkutsk to take a boat trip on the lake, though an American I met on my return journey who had done this assured me that it was a swindle, only two hours on the lake, and only a very restricted area covered. He also said Irkutsk was awful.

However, I did not see Irkutsk at all, for this was the day when I was suddenly taken ill, and could not get off the train when we arrived there. I had a gruelling attack of diarrhoea brought on either by the bottles of unsterilized milk I bought at station stalls or by the everlasting compote served up in a tumbler after every meal.

The attack so exhausted me that I slept most of the day. Indeed I think I must have been unconscious part of the time, in a deep swoon, because the old gentleman was most concerned about me when I finally staggered to my feet again. He was so concerned that he spoke to me in English:

'Are you ill?'

Even then, in my dire predicament, I noticed that he used British English and said 'ill', not 'sick', as a Japanese, accustomed to American

English, would have done. He spoke again, again using British English:
'Are you all right?'

I nodded weakly in reply to his question, and rubbed my sore stomach. At once he produced some tablets and made me swallow two. After a short while I felt very much better, and the dull aches left my exhausted joints. The train girl came along and asked if I wanted to see a doctor. There was no doctor on the train, but it might be possible to call one at the next big stop, about five hours away. Foreigners falling ill in Russia are supposed to get free treatment, but I doubt whether this is so: the Russians do not like to give anything away for nothing, and in any case when I looked for medications in Moscow I found severe shortages of the simplest things, and others impossible to obtain. I said I would not need a doctor. Everyone was most concerned about me. But I felt quite safe in charge of the old man. When they asked me what I thought was the cause of my illness, I said I had been drinking the unpasteurized milk sold at wayside stations, and they all cried out in alarm and distress. I was told never to drink such milk, and naturally enough I never did so again. I slept and slept, and by the next day I was well once more.

After Lake Baikal another great river, the Angara, leading to forested mountains. Then, towards evening, a shattering thunderstorm, slashing rain, gusts of cyclonic wind that made the train rock and bounce even more, blinding flashes of lightning, thunderbolts right overhead. I wondered if we were well insulated, and took care to keep my feet off the floor, though I am never quite sure whether this is the right thing to do. Perhaps it is better to have one's feet on the floor, then the lightning can pass right through one, like a dose of salts or the balls on some pinball machines that run straight through without touching a thing. The fierce storm lasted more than an hour, and seemed to be deliberately following the train. It was like being in a ship during a tempest. When it was over I had a long, good sleep.

Fifth day, Friday, 15th July. I awoke at six feeling fine. After the storm the sky was brilliantly blue. At a wayside stop, waiting for the train girl to stoke up the boiler with birch twigs and charcoal for my morning tea, I strolled on the deep country platform of a hamlet not yet awake, relishing the cool mist-laden air. All round the pretty little wooden station with its white palings, the spectral silver birches were haunting the mist with their utmost stillness, harbouring unknown to themselves the first faint chorus of wakening birds. I felt a longing to leave the train there and then, and set off strolling over the steppes, kicking the wet grass until the toes of my shoes were gilded with the plastered petals of buttercups.

But the girl called me from my dreams and back to the train, which had began to slide gently, swiftly, silently away behind my back. I sat down on my strapontin in the still empty corridor. With a toothless smile that was always curiously sweet in his sooty, wrinkled old face, the girl's father brought me my first glass of fresh, steaming tea, comforting and refreshing. It was boiling hot, so I cooled it down to the right temperature with some vodka. As I sipped and paused, sipped and paused, I gazed out of the grime-smeared window at that beautiful and awesome land, and felt for a moment supremely happy.

I am happy too, reading Gorky's great stories in the collection called *Through Russia*. What eyes he had for life, and what ears! There are frequent descriptions of the sound of church bells in this marvellous artist's work—a sound never heard now. I believe it is a sound he would have missed very much in the villages and towns I am passing through—drab and featureless, with never a steeple-house.

We rumbled for about five minutes over bridges spanning the River Iya—a very broad, tranquil river. Along its banks patient horses with high-hooped harnesses were dragging low carts, languorously urged on by suntanned youths, hair bleached white, wearing rubber boots and faded brown trousers patched with white. A sense of perfect rusticity and apartness: their faces are expressionless as they look at the passing train. No one waves. They do not wave to us, just look at us through narrowed eyes as they scratch their bare chests bright with pale yellow curls.

As we approach Novosibirsk the green, rolling steppes are like the Berkshire Downs, only vaster, with clumps of trees composed of firs and silver birch instead of beech and oak.

Now reapers are scything the meadows all along the tracks, cutting down with the lank, rich hay the clustering galaxies of wild flowers—meadowsweet, huge moons of cow parsley, towers of wild lupins, hedges of wild roses, splashes of sunflowers' wild yellow and tobacco-brown, pink candytuft, patches of misty blue and violet and mauve, all blooming and seeming almost to sing with the blissful intensity and sweet passion of the brief, all too brief, summer. These fields might truly have been described by a poet like Charles Cotton as 'enamelled' fields. They have a Pre-Raphaelite richness, freshness and innocence as the breeze stirs them before they feel the severer breeze of the mowers' keen-bladed scythes. I am reminded of Marvell's lines from 'The Mower's Song':

> ... But these, while I with sorrow pine,
> Grew more luxuriant still and fine;
> That not one blade of grass you spied,
> But had a flower on either side ...

Now the haycocks are going up all over the place, simple heaps just like our English ones, but always with a few silver birch branches laid over the top in the direction of the prevailing westerly wind. I see not a single mowing-machine: it is all done by hand, and every nook and corner of the fields and the railway embankments is harvested and gleaned with scythes, sickles and rakes. I feel the movement of the summer steppe itself as one immense swing of a gigantic scythe, that swing so hard to acquire, but which, when mastered, sends the curved blade of the scythe flickering close to the ground like a silver serpent or a migrating eel.

I saw only one, presumably communal, tractor, pulling a huge load of green hay, stopped at a railway crossing. Two boys, like Tom Sawyer and Huckleberry Finn, lay at their ease on top of the load, chewing straws, their Jackie Coogan caps pulled well down over their eyes.

My philosopher friend gets off here, at Novosibirsk, I shall miss him. I ask if I may write to him, but after a moment's hesitation he says no. I ask if I may take his picture. He again says no. This was my experience with all Russians, but it is not a sinister one I am sure. They simply see no point in prolonging what was only a passing intimacy; unlike the volatile Filipinos who beg one for one's address and never write, the Russians are honest: they know they will never write, so why bother? And it is not only the Russians who dislike having their pictures taken by strangers.

So I shook hands gently with the old man and helped him with his bags. On the platform, he suddenly flung his arms round me, hugged me and kissed me on both cheeks. I did the same to him. Then he departed without a word, a small, frail figure in a little embroidered skull-cap, weighed down by two suitcases full of books and papers, met by no one.

There were plenty of people on the animated station platform who had come to meet passengers getting off the train. They had brought with them sheaves of wild flowers, bunches of gladioli, armfuls of rambler roses to present in greeting to their returning friends and relatives. There were happy cries, bursts of laughter, long embraces, fervent kissings, tears of emotion. My own eyes filled with tears of joy at the sight of so much natural human warmth and affection. During my first few days in Siberia I had began to think that the Russians were utterly lacking in finer feelings. Until I got on the train most of them had certainly given me the cold shoulder and the sharp edge of their tongues. Perhaps as one moves westward, away from the extremes of Asian Russia, temperaments become gentler. That is what I am hoping. . . .

As I am stretching my legs on the platform someone runs up to me and thrusts a huge bouquet of purple and yellow lupins into my arms. It is given me by a pretty girl beside whom I sat once or twice in the restaurant-car. We talked in French, and she had told me she was training to be a ballerina at a school in Novosibirsk. She must have been quite famous, for a huge crowd of fellow students had come to greet her. She was loaded with huge bunches of flowers, just like a ballerina at the end of a successful performance.

'See you in *Swan Lake*!' I called to her, waving and smiling as the train began to move away. She and all her companions waved back. But it was a false alarm; the train was not starting yet, though its slight movement had caused some panic among the queues of men, women and children around the ice-cream vendors. Having dashed to the train, they dashed back to the ice-cream, buying up dozens of tubs at a time. What was amusing, and revealing, was the way the purchasers would clutch the tubs of cheap choc-flavoured ice-cream to their bosoms and run away to their compartments at top speed, as if terrified their spoils would be snatched from them by envious passers-by. They had the harsh acquisitive instinct of wild animals hunting in a rude and desperate society in which, just as everywhere else, it was every man for himself, only more so!

Judging by the people I saw at Novosibirsk, the Russians seem to have, and to be set on obtaining, the essentials of life. Most are decently dressed, but there is no sense of style or smartness or elegance, no variety; they all look alike and dress alike.

Novosibirsk is a big modern town on a wide river, the Ob'. Like many new Russian towns, it is closed to tourists, but this is simply, I think, because there is no suitable accommodation for visitors. From the train I could see many fine modern streets with blocks of new apartments *ad infinitum*. But there were also clusters of broken-down wooden shanties in small ravines just outside the town. There were scores of people fishing from the banks of the river: again trying to get something for nothing, a little river fish to add variety to a dull diet. There were the usual silver-painted and very pedestrian statues of Peace at the station. The train drove on into the slow twilight. As we are travelling westwards, the evenings seem to get longer and longer, dusk is hours in falling, and time seems to have stopped altogether. My circadian rhythm is disrupted.

I share my compartment now with a Russian family: young husband and plump, apparently older, wife, with two boys.

Next stop Omsk! I am reminded by this name of a curiously interesting book about Russia which I read some years ago.[1] I remember it was full of odd details about Russia and other Iron Curtain countries, and bright with a lively prejudice. On to Omsk!

[1] *Don't Send Me To Omsk!* by Roy Macgregor-Hastie. Macdonald, London, 1961.

4
MOSCOW TIME

THE family that got into my compartment at Novosibirsk appeared to be a typical Russian family. They seemed almost unreal, for they were so normal in every way, so healthy and solid. It was like a Noah's Ark family, completely ordinary, completely lacking in mystery.

Again I am conscious of this lack of decadence, this absence of mystery, in modern Russians. Have they become superhuman machines? I look again at Evgeny Evtushenko's poem, 'Mysteries', in the prose translation given in *The Penguin Book of Russian Verse*, which I have also brought with me:

> The mysteries of adolescence melt like mists by the shore ... Tonyas and Tanyas were mysteries, even with chapped legs.
>
> Stars and animals were mysteries, and so were clumps of mushrooms beneath the aspens; and doors creaked mysteriously: only in our childhood do they creak like this.
>
> The riddles of the universe appeared like balls out of the mouth of a fascinating conjurer, who fascinates us to good effect ...
>
> Enchanted snowflakes descended on the fields and the woods; enchanted sparks of laughter danced in the eyes of the girls.
>
> Mysteriously we whispered things to each other on the mysterious ice of the skating-rink; and timidly, like mystery touching mystery, hand touched hand.
>
> But suddenly adulthood came. The conjurer, his tail-coat worn to tatters, departed like a touring player to a far-away land, to perform in someone else's childhood.
>
> We grown-ups are forgotten by him. Oh, conjurer, you're a bad man! Woefully unmysterious, the snow falls on our shoulders.
>
> Where are you, magic balls? When we feel sad, it is unmysteriously. Other people are unmysterious for us, and we are unmysterious for them ...
>
> And if by chance one hand touches another, stroking it lightly, it's only a hand, not a mystery, don't you see?—only a hand!
>
> Give me a mystery—just a plain and simple one—a mystery which is diffidence and silence, a slim little, barefoot mystery: give me a mystery—just one!

This poem expresses perfectly my own feelings about modern Russia. In a sense it tells the truth about the whole of our modern world, a world increasingly devoid of mystery, a universe in which even the moon has been defiled by scientific equipment. The only mystery left to us today, in a scientific civilization where even the soul has been weighed and found wanting, is the presence in our skies and on our earth of unidentified flying objects and men from space, our cosmic brothers from other worlds far more advanced than ours. One day they will reveal themselves to us completely, and we shall love them for their mystery, their difference, their nobility and grace and love of peace. A few months later I was to see my first U.F.O. in Russian skies—above the Kremlin in Moscow. But that story must wait until my final chapter.

This family showed me how necessary it is to be normal and ordinary. Without such people life could not go on. They showed me that the everyday is the basis for fantasy and imagination. As Boris Pasternak's Dr Zhivago says in his diary: 'The fabulous is never anything but the commonplace touched by the hand of genius.'

Pasternak was certainly a genius, though an imperfect one: his work is shapeless and flawed in many places, yet the essential Russian goodness of the man shines out of everything he writes. That goodness, with its childlike quality, was something I sensed in the family in my compartment. Pasternak himself loved this quality of childlike innocence that seems to be the essential character of every good Russian, just as it is of every good Japanese. Zhivago again writes in his diary: 'What I have come to like best in the whole of Russian literature is the childlike Russian quality of Pushkin and Chekhov.'

That heavenly childlike innocence is a quality much needed in a world without mystery, a life without a soul.

After we passed through Omsk at ten o'clock, the two boys, sturdy, good-natured, well-behaved and intelligent chaps, were put to bed together in the bunk above mine. They were allowed to read quietly to each other for fifteen minutes before their father switched off their reading light on the dot, as he warned them he would do. There were no complaints from the boys, who obediently went to sleep at once.

The husband and wife and I had nodded and smiled to each other, but they were too busy putting their things in order to take much notice of me. Then the man spoke to me, and I realized they thought I was Russian, because they spoke in Russian. I said in Russian:

'I am English. I do not speak Russian.'

They were astonished and delighted.

'But you *do* speak Russian!' cried the father in Russian, with a beaming smile.

'No, I do not speak Russian,' I said again in Russian.

We all burst out laughing at this comic situation, in which I was using my few words of Russian to say that I could not speak Russian. When they laughed the husband and wife displayed perfect, regular, white teeth in suntanned faces. I thought I had never seen a healthier and more attractive couple. They were not exactly good looking, but radiated vitality and intelligence; these things are more important to me than conventional good looks. In fact I dislike and distrust anyone who is too good looking: usually such people have nothing else to recommend them.

We began talking in English and German. The wife said:

'Ah! Englishman! That is good. We love England. President Wilson.'

'Prime Minister Wilson,' I corrected her gently.

'Gentleman. English gentleman,' she went on radiantly. 'Shakespeare, Byron, Dickens, Oscar Wilde, Bertrand Russell, Arnold Wesker.'

I was surprised that she knew about Wesker. But in fact his plays have been translated into Russian and are often performed.

I discovered that she was a school-teacher and her husband a geologist. He was very interested in the stones—a kind of garnet, I believe—on my Japanese cufflinks. They assumed that I was married and had a family. Why shouldn't they? That was their normal way of life, and they could not conceive of a man without a wife and children and home. I told them I was a vagabond, with no family ties, no wish to settle down.

'Have you a girl friend? A girl friend very lovely Japanese girl?' the husband asked politely.

'No,' I replied. 'My only girl friend was English. We were going to be married. She was blown to pieces by a German bomb in an air raid on London in 1945. I have no desire to marry anyone else. I prefer to be alone.'

While his wife was out in the lavatory, preparing for the night, he drew close to me and whispered:

'But how do you manage? Do you masturbate?'

'Not if I can help it,' I replied quickly, and we both laughed heartily in a man-to-man fashion, while he slapped me on the back and produced a bottle of plum brandy. We were soon toasting each other every few minutes. The Russian capacity for strong drink almost exceeds my own, but they often seem unable to hold their liquor. I had seen, and was to see, reeling drunkards very frequently in the streets and parks of the Soviet Union. We downed one small glass after another: the plum brandy was not to be sipped delicately; it had to be tossed off at one gulp, and followed by a gulp of water. Soon I had that delicious floating sensation which just the right amount of good drink, taken in pleasant company, produces in me.

They asked about my C.N.D. badge, and I explained to them my membership of Bertrand Russell's Campaign for Nuclear Disarmament. I told them I had been a conscientious objector during World War Two, and that I had been forced to work as a labourer in camps in England for five years.

This information actually brought tears to their eyes, and they both embraced me passionately. After a brief discussion between them in Russian, they presented me with a large silver coin of great beauty, officially worth one rouble, which had been struck to commemorate the Russian entry into Berlin at the end of the war. It was a noble coin, with the Sword of Stalingrad engraved on one side. I managed to smuggle it out of the country as a souvenir, though I realized it is strictly forbidden by Russian authorities to take out any Russian money. But I think this coin was an exception. At any rate I made it so.

We made a final toast: 'Long live Anglo-Soviet friendship!' Then we undressed and went to sleep.

Sixth day, Saturday, 16th July. A straightforward sunrise: no complications, no clouds, no great dramatic surprises. The huge deep orange sun rose over the steppe into an empty sky. It was like a natural birth, with no pain and no mess, and reminded me of Gorky's marvellous story about childbirth, in *Through Russia*.

There are sometimes small white goats in the fields, and large herds of cattle.

I am spellbound by the beauty of the silver birches in the sunrise. Here their foliage seems denser, hanging in heavy clouts and rags of green. I remember Robert Frost's poem:

> When I see birches bend to left and right
> Across the lines of straighter darker trees,
> I like to think some boy's been swinging them.
> But swinging doesn't bend them down to stay.
> Ice-storms do that . . .

> You may see their trunks arching in the woods
> Years afterwards, trailing their leaves on the ground
> Like girls on hands and knees that throw their hair
> Before them over their heads to dry in the sun . . .
>
> One could do worse than be a swinger of birches . . .

They remind me of the silver birches I used to love when I lived in Sweden, and which I describe in my poem entitled 'Jämtland' from *The Prodigal Son*:

> The silver birch is papery, and veils
> Its elbowed branches gloved with black
> In a suspended shower of golden scales,
> Its own slight leaves, that pattern a forest track
> Like narrow starshine's riddled flakes
> Or coins struck from the moonlight's hidden lakes . . .

The birches are fine for paper-making. Here the miles upon miles of four-barred fencing are constructed entirely of birch boughs. In cottage gardens there is nearly always a nesting-box for wild birds set on a tall post, and to the box are always nailed one or two bare branches of silver birch, to encourage the birds to alight there and use the little home so kindly provided.

This is my last full day on the train, but so far I have seen no dramatic changes of landscape. Always the rolling steppe rolls on, with its tall grass, wild flowers and rustic mowers, whose graceful, rhythmical movements with their glittering scythes remind me of another Frost poem, 'Mowing':

> There was never a sound beside the wood but one,
> And that was my long scythe whispering to the ground . . .
> The fact is the sweetest dream that labour knows.
> My long scythe whispered and left the hay to make.

There is something very like Russia in such poems by Frost: the same virgin, childlike quality, the same freshness and wholesomeness and sanity. I am sure he must be popular in Russia.

At large stations there are platform trucks laden with what at first sight look like lumps of dirty snow, but on closer inspection I find that they are slowly melting chunks of river ice preserved all winter and spring for summer use. They are stained brownish-yellow. People are buying the uncouth lumps and washing them under a stand-pipe.

After Novosibirsk and Omsk, station supplies become richer and more varied: besides the universal ice-cream, I can now find at station stalls beer, roast chickens and several kinds of cakes. But they are all very expensive. I paid about fourteen shillings for half a roast chicken, which was wrapped up for me in dirty newspaper. At every stop, passengers are filling empty milk or beer bottles with fresh water from stand-pipes, for there is no drinking water on the train, and carafes of water are never placed on the tables in the dining-car.

Between Tcheliabinsk and Sverdlovsk the first few television aerials appear on the roofs of country cottages. We must now be passing through the famous Urals, but they are so insignificant on this vast open visage of this immense plain that they have gone before I notice them. At Sverdlovsk, people were buying *Izvestiya* from newspaper vending machines. Crowds were thronging the bookstalls, hoping to pick up some new Moscow editions.

Outside this fine city there is a beautiful stretch of water, the Iset River, a tributary of the Tobol, set in verdant hills and vales, a conifer country. A new air of animation has seized everyone in the train, as if they could all smell Moscow coming nearer and nearer: we shall be there tomorrow!

The geologist has bought at Sverdlovsk station a bottle of excellent Tirnovo, a warm, full-bodied, semi-sweet wine from Bulgaria, almost a Marsala or Muscatel. We share the bottle, toasting the future. One of the accordionists from the Bolshoi Circus comes to the door with his instrument and begins playing us some thrilling Russian folk-dances. Everyone gathers round, singing and clapping hands. It's a wild scene. The old man and his daughter the train girl come along to see what all the uproar is about, and we toast them too, and make them share a glass of wine, something the old man consents to do only behind closed doors; apparently it is forbidden to drink while on duty, but who cares? Rules are meant to be broken, and what the eye doesn't see the heart doesn't grieve over. The old man toasts me, and I toast him in return. I have become very fond of him. I shall never forget his sweet, worn face. He is like a piece of Old Russia, with his wide smile in his charcoal-smeared, rough-stubbled face, a smile made curiously more jovial by the one blackened fang on the right-hand side of the upper jaw. I like his thick, bushy, black, down-sweeping eyebrows, deep-furrowed grey cheeks, scanty, whitening hair. His sweetness and simplicity seem essentially Russian. I thank him for his constant kindness to me, brewing me two glasses of tea every morning; however early I get up he is always up before me, lighting the charcoal in the water heater at the end of the corridor. I shall always think of him with affection—so self-effacing, so modest, so undemanding. To me, he represents the true soul of Russia. I was touched when his daughter came up to me unexpectedly, and said, blushing all over her open, healthy face: 'I understand your heart.'

Why did she say that, I wondered. She is a university student who spends her holidays working on the train with her father, partly to help him, for he is getting beyond the work, and partly to earn a little pocket-money for her studies. She speaks fair English, and is studying to be a biologist. A delightful, straightforward creature, honest as the day. She reminds me, in her simplicity and honesty, of some of my students at Japan Women's University, though she is more boyish and more outspoken than they could ever be.

I keep wondering why she said to me: 'I understand your heart'.

Most of the other Soviet women on the train were equally honest and frank: they were often monumentally large, like the figures of Fernand Léger and Picasso's massive-footed giantesses.

Though I am happy with these Russians, I feel sorry that there are no Japanese on the train. I miss Japan very much, and my heart aches with nostalgia for the special fragrance of the Japanese soul, and for the gay bars of Shinjuku. However, on my return trip through Russia by train to Tokyo, I was to meet two excellent Japanese gentleman. The first, Tadashi Kitagawa, is a brilliant young pianist studying in Copenhagen, where his wife is harpist with the Danish Symphony Orchestra. I met him on the train from Warsaw to Brest and Moscow. He invited me to the piano recital he gave in April at the Festival Hall in Ueno Park, a recital graced by a beautiful performance of a piece by one of my favourite Russian composers, Scriabin.

The other Japanese was a representative of the Trade Department of Sankyo Bussan Co. Ltd, Tsuneo Hirano, who had been on a business trip to Moscow. His company on the train and on the *Baikal* was particularly welcome to me, because he could speak fluent Russian. Both of these Japanese made excellent travelling companions.

The next stop after Sverdlovsk was Perm. Here huge jars of tomato purée were on sale, as they had been at Sverdlovsk station, and there were actually fresh tomatoes too, something I had not seen since leaving Japan. But there were such hordes of excited people queuing for these rather inferior-looking tomatoes that I thought it was not worth the bother. I spent three kopeks on sweet, sickly fizz from a machine. The platforms at Perm were very animated, and it was amusing to watch the acrobats walking about on their hands, or

The Amur beach at Khabarovsk

Khabarovsk

Small ads for private sales, part-time jobs and apartments to let

A corner of Komsomol Square

The Trans-Siberian Railway at Novosibirsk

'There are plenty of people on the animated station platform'

Girl gymnasts of the Bolshoi in track-suits

The Trans-Siberian Railway at Novosibirsk

One man's poise. Bolshoi Circus acrobat keeps fit at every short stop

Fruit drinks stall. 'I spent three kopecks on sweet sickly fizz'

Moscow

Soldiers of the Red Army touring the Kremlin

Outside a baker's shop

Moscow

Theatre ticket kiosk. 'I was always able to get a ticket for some kind of show or concert'

Manège Square and a Kremlin spire from the Lenin Library

Leningrad

Soldiers look across the Neva from the Krasnovo-Flota quay towards the University and the Academies of Science and Fine Arts

Peter the Great—'The Bronze Horseman' in Decembrists' Square. Sculptor, Etienne-Maurice Falconet (1716–91)

Stockholm

Hippies at the steps of the Concert House. Sculptor of Poseidon and figures, Carl Miles (1875–1955)

Trans-Siberian Railway

Footballer at Shimanovskaya station. Sculptor unknown

balancing on one hand, amid the milling throngs of travellers, women station labourers, wheel-tappers, water-suppliers, ice-cream vendors and soldiers, all of whom took not the slightest notice of the acrobats wandering around on their hands.

There was a lake just north of Perm, and an immense river. Don or Volga? My knowledge of Russian geography is abysmal, and I have lost my map. Perm was the first city since leaving Khabarovsk in which I saw, on a river bank in the distance, something looking like an old onion or turnip-domed tower, perhaps a church steeple. At the station, just before the train left, I managed to buy with my few remaining roubles a bottle of 1959 vintage Hungarian wine—Tokaji Furmint, which I had often purchased and enjoyed in Tokyo, at the excellent wine department of Isetan Department Store. But in Russia it was rather a rarity, as the geologist told me. I shared the bottle with him and his wife just before dinner. He read me some extracts in Russian from *The Penguin Book of Russian Verse*: an amateur poetry recital, but one he made thrilling for me with his deep rich voice and dynamic sense of rhythm. I think all Russians must be natural readers of poetry, just as all Japanese are natural writers of poetry. He read me poems which he said he had not looked at since his schooldays, and which brought tears to his eyes—Byliny's ancient epic about Nightingale the Robber, and poems by Lomonosov, a fable by Krylov, an elegiac lyric by Zhukovsky, and bits of Lermontov and Pushkin and a love poem by Tyutchev. His wife and children sat listening to him in breathless silence. He seemed like a man carried away, right out of himself, right out of this world and time. Tears glittered in their eyes, and ran slowly down their cheeks. Though I could not understand, I sensed the great beauty of Russian verse in that simple, unaffected reading, and, perhaps encouraged also by the excellent wine, tears began pouring from my own eyes too. He stopped reading and we suddenly looked clear-eyed at each other's wet faces, and began laughing happily.

I pointed out to the geologist that the anthology was dedicated to the memory of Boris Pasternak. He nodded gravely and said nothing. He simply turned to the selection from Pasternak and read the wonderful poem about the steppe:

> How wonderful were those sallies into the stillness! The boundless steppe is like a sea-scape. The feather-grass sighs, the ants rustle, and the mosquitoes' whine drifts through the air . . .

He read more: Nekrasov and Bunin, Blok and Mayakovsky, and

finally, at my own request, one of my favourite modern Russian poets, Sergei Esenin, his beautiful *Letter to my Mother*:

> They write to tell me that, though you hide your anxiety, you're pining for me ever so much, and that you often come out on the road to look for me, wearing your worn old-fashioned coat . . .

This heart-breaking poem always reminds me of my own mother, she who is now patiently waiting for my return to England, after long years of absence. . . .

Hayricks in this part of Russia are built round a central pole, like those in Scandinavian countries. The evenings seem to be getting longer and longer, the shadows from the setting sun over the immense plains more and more poignant. There seems to be no more true darkness. Even at midnight the sky still glows. The 'white nights' of the Russian summer. The big red sun's ever slower declension over Kirov—the river, mists, smog, factory chimneys scrawling smoke across the vast, simple blue sky. Everyone is gathered excitedly round a small portable radio, listening to the broadcast of the U.S.S.R. versus Italia football match in the World Cup Series. It is obvious from the shouts of rapture from the Russians that their own team is winning. This puts them in an excellent temper for the evening meal. Another example of their simple childishness perhaps. One of the acrobats asks me what I think of the result, and a look of deep, uncomprehending shock spreads over his face when I say: 'Sport is boring.'

At Kirov station I saw two strange girls in mini-skirts and dyed hair stalking defiantly round the platforms on high heels, followed by the wondering gazes of their suspicious compatriots. Where had they got those clothes? This was obviously the question in everyone's mind. Another odd-looking girl at the station, curiously bony and angular, and with very large feet stuffed into tiny pointed shoes, face crudely made up, looked like a 'blue boy', but I had no time to investigate.

At Kirov we turn our watches four hours back, from 12 p.m. to 8 p.m.—Moscow time!

Before we compose ourselves for sleep on this last night on the train we drink vodka and make toasts:

'Long life to the Union of Soviet Socialist Republics!' I cry, downing a fiery mouthful of my favourite drink.

'Long live Lenin!' Another glassful tossed off like so much water.

'Long live Anglo-Soviet friendship!' the wife suddenly cries, slightly flushed with drink and glowing all over with goodwill.

'Long live world peace and the friendship of all nations!' I counter, swallowing another dose. 'Long live Pasternak! Long live Evtuschenko! Long live Andrey Voznesensky!'

Glasses were raised again and again. Finally, I cried:

'Long live Sino-Soviet friendship! Long live Chairman Mao!'

This outburst created a certain chilly silence, but only for a moment. We were soon off again, toasting everyone we could think of until after midnight. The sky outside the dusty windows was still light.

Seventh day, Sunday, 17th July. About three hours' sleep. I woke to the first pearly dawn light at just after three-thirty, to find my face and hair once more—but for the last time—strewn with a fine net of soot and cinders. Even my navel is full of dust and ash. My hair is now stiff with soot, and I feel I shall never be clean again. With relief I raised my head for the last time from that filthy pillow.

3.45 a.m. The sun slowly rising above dark forests of foliage in which the slender trunks of silver birches can just be seen glimmering like young girls' naked thighs or the breastless, sexless torsos and raised, ghostly thin arms of wood-nymphs. The huge disc of the sun looks corroded, like a lump of red-hot iron, dusted with ashes, scarred with impurities, gradually being brought to white heat in the cloudless furnace of the morning skies.

Teams of women mowers in boots and headscarves are already scything the dewy meadows that are still dark under the trees. Long flights of crows swooping over the swathes of fresh hay. Some of these big black birds stalk the sun-shot metals of the dark rails, others titubate on glossy telegraph wires, making a constant seesawing movement with their clumsy tails to preserve their comic equilibrium.

4.30 a.m. A brief stop at Buy. I enjoy the cool freshness of the morning air on the little station platform, smelling of hay and pines and soup. Some passengers get off the train and stroll about in pyjamas, doing vague exercises, taking deep breaths of this delicious air. The station is an elegant, Greek-pillared building painted white and lime green. On the smooth, log-laden river four fisherman in four narrow, pointed boats are fishing in the shadows of the girdered bridge.

We trundle past small stations overshadowed by high octagonal water-towers of blackened brick, which with their inverted bell-flower roofs, look like medieval basilicas round which swifts and swallows are flickering and flirting with bats. Jackdaws stand like ornaments on the parapets of stone station buildings; one of them is peering with tilted, intelligent head, right down a wide, low, brick chimney.

We flashed through stations with little dark green gardens and shrubberies in which the *blafard*, big, silver-painted bust of Lenin, always moons and dodges among the leaves like a ghost.

At Jaroslav, the Volga. All the passengers at the windows, adoring silently this greatest and most famous of all the great Russian rivers. I take some pictures of it from the moving train as we cross on an endless bridge. Of that view of Jaroslav I remember a church by the river with a group of rust-red turnip-domes. Then, on the other bank, an eighteenth-century church, exquisite, with an infinitely slender spire. I snapped these unsuccessfully. I should say here that I took pictures quite freely everywhere in Russia. No one seemed to think it out of order for me to photograph scenes from the windows of the train or on the station platforms. Only once, on my return journey through Russia, did I have any trouble about taking pictures. It was on the station of a small town, Shimanovskaya, where I was trying to photograph some interesting statuary commemorating someone who appeared to be a local hero. An unpleasant lout, a tall worker all in black with a sullen face came up to me shouted incomprehensibly. But I got his drift. I smiled and answered:

'I'm sorry I don't speak Russian.'

He gave me another glare and a growl, and for a moment I thought he was going to attack me. However, he lurched slowly away along the tracks to join some other workmen. I did not look back, but strolled very slowly along the platform of this extremely pretty station and climbed nonchalantly into the train, relieved at not being pursued. My fellow passengers, some of whom had witnessed the encounter, made no comment.

At Zagorsk, about one hour from Moscow, the train flashes by a sudden extraordinary vision of turnip-shaped domes, azure, covered with large golden stars. Above them rises a magnificent rococo tower. Coming after thousands of miles of more or less featureless landscape, the effect of those gorgeous domes and noble tower was electrifying. Everyone ran to the windows, exclaiming at their Byzantine beauty. What I had seen, as if in a vision of heaven, was the famous Trinity-Saint Sergius Monastery, one of the most remarkable examples of ancient Russian religious architecture, built mostly by Ivan the Terrible, comparable with the Lavra in Kiev and the Theraponte

Monastery near Vologda. The vast church at the centre of the monastery is the Cathedral of the Dormition. Under its five blue-and-gold, bulb-shaped towers lies the tomb of Boris Godunov, and there is a miraculous fountain from which pilgrims draw water. The great tower I had glimpsed was the 290-feet high belfry designed by the celebrated architect Rastrelli. It is as magnificent as the best seventeenth-century Italian campaniles. Peter the Great took shelter here in 1685 during the revolt of the *streltsy* and Catherine II confiscated part of its wealth and land. But the monastery still possessed fabulous treasures on the outbreak of the 1917 Revolution, after which the property was nationalized and converted into a museum. However, after the Second World War nearly all the churches in the great complex of buildings were reopened for worship.

This month of July 1966 there is a special pilgrimage to Zagorsk in celebration of the three hundredth anniversary of the birth of St Sergius.

Then we were approaching the outskirts of Moscow.

When I got off the train my Intourist guide, a young man chewing gum, was waiting for me on the platform. He informed me that I had been booked into the Minsk Hotel in Gorky Street. ('Very nice comfortable convenient modern,' he rattled off.) In Russia, one cannot choose at what hotels one will stay: one simply has to go where Intourist puts one. I saw the hippie from America, surrounded by all the admiring Russian friends he had made on the train. They were saying hasty goodbyes. I too said goodbye to him. He was not staying the night in Moscow, but making for Stockholm as fast as possible, there to catch an Icelandic air-liner, the cheapest mode of transportation to the States. I shook hands with him and with the old man who had been such a kind attendant on the train. I also said goodbye to his young daughter, who hugged me, kissed me on both cheeks, and said, tears in her eyes: 'I understand your heart.' The best part of my trip to Russia was ended.

PART THREE

HORRORSVILLE

I

MOSCOW MULES

Moscow, I saw at once, is Horrorsville. The Minsk Hotel in Gorky Street looks from the outside like a fine modern place, with lots of sheet glass and two restaurants. There is no night-club and no bar, but a number of souvenir shops selling, for American dollars only, vodka furs, amber, caviar, cigarettes and badges of all kinds.

I had a nice little room, with bath, overlooking a quiet back street of old-fashioned brick apartment houses. However, it was not insulated against the constant sound of doors banging all along the corridor, at the end of which was permanently enthroned one of the nastier institutions of Russian hotel life, a domineering matriarch in charge of the room keys and the samovar. She spoke only Russian, and her face of stone with its hard little eyes never once smiled. She was a real Gorgon, and I could feel my blood freeze every time I walked to my room.

I had often read that there are no plugs in Soviet bathrooms and had always felt this must simply be malicious anti-Russian propaganda at work. But both in Khabarovsk and in Moscow my wash-basin had no plug. There was a tiny square bath which did indeed have a plug, but it did not fit the hole and so the water soon ran out. With the help of my nail-scissors I managed to detach it from the bath and use it in the basin, which it also did not fit. But it kept some water in the basin for a fair length of time, enough to rub through my smalls. It was only later that I was to discover the great value of the gilt screw-top metal cup provided so thoughtfully on the half-bottle flask by the makers of Old Parr whisky. This makes a perfect stopper which fits every kind of hole in Soviet baths and basins.

Next morning, when I returned for lunch, I saw that my room maid had carefully tied the plug and chain on the bath again, with a piece of strong wire which I could not loosen.

Here, as in Khabarovsk, there was a steam-heated towel-rack in the bathroom, a luxury unheard of in most Asian and European hotels. Unfortunately it heated the entire room to the point of suffocation, and we were already in the height of the Moscow summer, which can be very hot. There was no means of turning off the towel-rack, and if I opened the double windows the din of the wretched dance band from the restaurant floated up, not to mention the flies from the kitchen. The toilet paper was a sort of light, stiff parchment, oblongs cut apparently from tracing-paper. My one towel was a small white damask tablecloth, with which it was impossible to get properly dry. The bed was the absolute minimum of length and comfort, the pillow thin. I had to make my own bed from bedding stowed away in a cupboard at the bed-end.

The first thing I did when entering the room was to twiddle the white plastic wheel under the base of the telephone and pull the tiny radio's plug out of the wall-socket. Then, addressing the ventilator, I shouted:

'Good morning, comrades! How are you? I know you are listening!'

Then I recited a stream of obscene words and phrases in Japanese, English, German, French, Italian and Spanish. On the train I had tried hard to find out from the other passengers some dirty Russian words and phrases, but without success: everyone seemed shocked by this aspect of my linguistic interests. However, from a Russian sailor I once encountered briefly in a Yokohama bar, I had learnt the Russian for one particularly opprobrious name, and this I shouted several times at the ventilator.

'You might also tell them to switch off this bloody hot towel-rack!' I concluded. Strangely enough, next day the towel-rack was switched off, to my great relief. I thanked the ventilator in Russian, then asked, in English, if I might have a plug for the wash-basin. This was also provided next day, attached to one of the taps by a padlock.

I tried to think of the reason for this lack of plugs. Is it due to the actual shortage of plugs, causing Russians staying in hotels to steal them for use in their own plugless apartments? Or is it that the Russians cannot be trusted to turn off the bathroom taps, and the hotel arranges things like this to prevent flooding? Actually after I had taken a shower the floor of my bathroom was inches deep in water!

The first time I sat on the toilet the plastic seat broke: the crack used to inflict savage little pinches on my bare bottom. I complained about this to the ventilator, but no action was taken.

It was a surprise, in such an apparently modern structure, to find such old, small, hot, creaking lifts, slow and not automatic, with heavy grilles that one had to use all one's strength to wrench open. I pressed the lift button to summon the lift, and the whole metal plate surrounding it fell off, bringing away with it part of the crumbling wall.

At the service centre in the lobby, where extremely unhelpful girls at various desks are supposed to arrange one's sightseeing and travel tickets, they refused to cash a traveller's cheque, giving as their excuse that it was a Sunday. Cheques can be cashed at other hotels like the Metropol and the National on Sundays, but you must go before 5 p.m. I was struck by the sheer disagreeableness of the staff at the reception desk. They had already had my passport for five hours; when I asked for it back, explaining that I needed it in order to cash my cheque, I was told I could not have it for another four hours, as it had not yet been 'processed'. (Two strange men had followed me to the reception desk on my arrival and peered over to scrutinize the passport when I handed it to the very cross woman clerk.) I insisted that I must have my passport back, as I had no roubles and wanted to buy some dinner. (Credit is never allowed in Russian hotels: one has to pay for what one has eaten at the end of every meal.) The woman clerk asked me, suspiciously, if I were a member of the British Industrial Exhibition delegation staying at the hotel and I said yes. With a vexed sigh she disappeared and brought me my passport within two minutes and handed it over unwillingly.

This is the general Russian attitude: determination *not* to do anyone a favour if it can possibly be avoided. I suppose it is a hard mentality created by successive shortages and by the battle to keep one's head above water, a battle in which one must show *no* weakness and not give an inch to anyone; in which one must always be on the look-out for one's own advantage. For people who feel they are being perpetually scored over, to be able to refuse even the slightest things to others is about the only luxury they can enjoy. It is this hard mentality, and the hard, unsmiling faces that go with it, that help to make Moscow into Horrorsville for the single, defenceless traveller. If one protests, all one gets in return is the Russian shrug and a contemptuous sneer.

It was such a business trying to get a few clothes washed and pressed. Neatly pressed trousers are not in evidence in Russia's totally undistinguished and dull male dress. The trousers were pressed very badly.

It takes literally hours to order breakfast and lunch, to wait for the food to appear on the table, and then to pay for it. The Riga beer—when one can get it, for often it is unobtainable—is good, but the food is just plain uninteresting. I have had much better Russian food in the Russian restaurants of Tokyo (though not at the Volga, an overrated and overpriced eatery near Tokyo Tower); the Sungari and the Ukraine restaurants in Shinjuku, and the delightfully situated Rogoski with its charming Russian staff on the ninth floor of the Tokyo Building in Shibuya, provide food infinitely better cooked and better served than anywhere in the Soviet Union.

I was amused by the conversation of two British commercial travellers attending the British Industrial Exhibition in Moscow. Apparently the hall where the exhibition is being held is overpoweringly hot and smelly. Said one:

'One thing we did notice yesterday, there aren't so many flies about now.'

'No, now that you mention it, there aren't, I suppose.'

I went wandering down Gorky Street, Moscow's main thoroughfare of shops, hotels, department stores and *gastronom*. Official guides, I was to find out later, always tell of how dirty and narrow it used to be and how it was widened, cleaned and improved after the revolution. The same thing is said about most of Moscow's very wide 'prospekts' which are certainly impressive in an impersonal, grandiose but architecturally humdrum, all too solid way. Gorky Street has some appalling examples of official Stalinesque architecture: huge, old-fashioned buildings from the thirties surmounted by enormous heroic statues: common without being vulgar.

There are still a few streets of old wooden one- or two-storey buildings just behind the triumphal arches of Gorky Street. Here too there are pretty little rococo churches with gilded turnip-domes, one or two dilapidated brick churches which had obviously been Protestant and brick houses colour-washed with brick colour, shaded by limes and aspens and silver birches. These are delightful, human streets where it is a pleasure to walk: but the tourists are never shown these parts, which are supposed to be 'unprogressive'.

The first impression given by Moscow, and by most Russian towns, is one of great expanses, spaciousness, calm. One sets off to cross one of those extremely wide streets as if departing on an expedition. The masses of Sunday humanity traipsing through these vast, somehow empty streets and boulevards seem tamed, hushed and overwhelmed by the repressive, inhuman proportions of their surroundings. One never hears laughter in the streets, or even conversation.

Many of the old churches in the narrow streets behind the main boulevards have been beautifully restored, and others are being renovated. But I saw one, made of brick, which was in ruins, weed-fringed, except for a great abandoned tower in a sort of north of England Primitive Methodist late-Victorian style. Nearly all churches were shut on my first Sunday in Moscow, excepting those used as museums. But passers-by, chiefly old women, would genuflect and cross themselves outside the main portal, with its locked and bolted iron gates.

One of the nice things about Moscow is that people live in the centre of the city, in elderly apartment blocks or wooden houses, not only in the absolutely appalling suburbs of impersonal block after block of flats, which, despite their well-regulated lawns and shrubbery, look like landscapes on the moon.

I walked down Gorky Street past the monumental statuary representing Pushkin, heavily bearded, in frock coat and rigid pants, looking meditative. There is a charming, flowery, tree-shaded square arranged round the statue. Here, on long summer afternoons, I read most of Mihajlo Mihajlov's extraordinary work, *Moscow Summer,* an outspoken view of Russian literary and intellectual life which caused a scandal when it was first issued in Yugoslavia, and resulted in this fine and courageous author's unjust arrest, trial and imprisonment.

At the far end of Pushkin Square stands Moscow's largest cinema, the Rossia, a rectangular edifice of glass and steel seating 2,500 people. It was showing that endless and turgid film of *War and Peace* whose stars I had encountered on the *Baikal*: a huge poster displaying their faces covered an entire wall near my hotel.

The region between Pushkin Square and Petrovka Street, I was interested to see, still has an old name, the curious Passion Boulevard; but this name comes from the passion of Christ, and from the monastery that used to stand here before being pulled down to make the pleasant, shady Naryshkin Gardens on the other side of the Rossia. Near by I noticed an imposing classical building in the style of a Greek temple. I learned that in 1812 it was the headquarters of the celebrated English Club where Tolstoy set several scenes of *War and Peace*. It is now apparently a hospital. Farther down the slope on the corner of

Petrovka Street was a large monastery with strange domes and belfries. Farther on a very steep slope where the trams grind slowly along leads to a street with another old name, Nativity Boulevard. It is good to find that these old names still exist in a city where streets are increasingly named after cosmonauts and politicians (though all references to Stalin have, of course, been discreetly wiped out).

Coming back to Gorky Street, farther down its curving slope is Sovietskaya Square or the Square of the Soviets, with Moscow City Hall on the right. In 1946 this building was moved 33 feet on rollers from its original site, as was a large four-storey apartment in Gorky Street weighing 23,000 tons, which was transported 160 feet during the reconstruction and widening schemes in this area. Sovietskaya Square is chiefly remarkable for the immense equestrian statue, the monument to Yuri Dolgoruki, on a high granite pedestal. This statue of the founder of Moscow was commissioned in 1947 for the eighth centenary of the capital, and is so huge that it took six years to complete. A small Georgian restaurant, the Aragvi, is worth a visit for its expensive Georgian dishes. There are also numbers of large bookshops in this area.

Yuri Dolgoruki, in medieval armour, his right arm extended, pigeon-haunted, is a noble sight at dawn, with the sun rising over the trees behind him. The gardens around him are very pleasant. Indeed Moscow has more lovely parks, squares, statuary, memorials and commemorative plaques than Paris and Vienna put together. The statuary, like this example in Sovietskaya Square, is usually of inhumanly vast dimensions, faintly intimidating and yet absurd. Much better are the many delicately carved portrait plaques on the walls of old apartments and houses. And over it all hangs what I might call, parodying T. S. Eliot, 'an atmosphere of Lenin's Tomb'.

Farther down the slope of Gorky Street I passed a number of female clothes shops, their windows tattily dressed with artificial flowers: artistic window displays such as one finds in Tokyo and Paris and London seem to be frowned upon in Russia: they would seem too frivolous in this land without caprice. But in the windows were old-fashioned dummies of incredible slimness wearing dresses such as could never be worn by the vast majority of Russian women. Other windows were full of very 'hatty' hats. But one never sees a Russian woman wearing a hat, at least not in summer. If they wear anything at all over their artlessly trimmed hair it is the universal headscarf, worn in various styles, mostly utilitarian.

There were long queues in the grocery stores for a wretched selection of tinned food, occasional poor, half-rotten fruit and tomatoes. Wine and vodka counters also had long queues. One counter was selling glasses of mineral water, evil-tasting, another glasses of Bulgarian Cabernet, which was excellent, and tumblers of Russian champagne, too sweet and gassy.

There were even longer queues in the street for ice-cream, mineral water, green plums, lengths of dress material, all sold at small stalls outside the large shops.

Inside the *gastronom* one must first queue at the counter to see what is available and to find out its price. Then one queues at the cash desk to buy a ticket for the goods one desires. Then back to the counter to queue for the purchase: the goods are usually thrown at one, unwrapped, by disgruntled attendants, and most products seem of poor quality.

2

AN ATMOSPHERE OF LENIN'S TOMB

THE view of the Kremlin from the slopes of Gorky Street is a strange one: the gilded turnip-domes seen in the distance through modernistic lamp-standards. But my first sight, even such an incongruous one, was a thrill. Beside all the fake heroism of the architecture surrounding me, the Kremlin looked authentic.

I wander farther down the slope, past the monumental post office, which I later inspected and found wanting: it has none of the amenities of Japanese and Filipino post offices, but reminded me rather of the post offices in Korea: strictly functional. Impossible, here, to sip tea, smoke *papyrosi,* idle, chat, comb one's hair or sleep. It is a melancholy place, like a tomb in a vast cave. People go there only with the intention of buying stamps and sending telegrams. It was so intimidating that when I went to a stamps counter, I asked for stamps in fear and trembling, like the British lady in war time, when everything was rationed, who approached one of our British autocrats of the post office counters and quavered:

'Would you have such a thing as a stamp?'

At the National Hotel on the corner of Gorky Street and Manège Square I stopped for a Screwdriver. Sometimes I had lunch at this hotel, in which the service, while still slow and inefficient, seemed just a trifle more pleasant and speedy than at the Minsk Hotel.

Manège Square or Manezhnaya Square is one of the many great squares in Moscow, which has its Sverdlov Square, Revolution Square and, to the north, beyond the Karl Marx Avenue, Dzerzhinsky Square and Nogina Square.

Manezhnaya Square can hardly be called a public square, for one is not allowed to cross its vast acreage, and traffic must drive round the outside. It is used for parades on May Day and on 7th November, the date of the anniversary of the Soviet Communist regime that was set up after the 'ten days that shook the world', and whose fiftieth anniversary was celebrated in 1967.

The Riding School, where Tolstoy learnt to bicycle, is a beautiful classic Greek-style building with an imposing portico and pediment. It was built in 1817 for the horse exercises of the Tsar's officers. I was hoping to see here a display similar to the one put on regularly at the baroque Spanish Riding School in Vienna, where, under crystal chandeliers, the white Lipizzaners courbette and capriole to the strains of Mozart and Johann Strauss. But the Manège in Moscow has now been turned into an exhibition hall: I was disappointed to find that a fine display devoted to the poet Esenin had just closed. After the Revolution this seat of Tsarist splendour was used as a garage for the Kremlin motor-cars.

There are two very charming eighteenth-century buildings near by, now housing the Arts Faculties of Moscow University, which was founded by the Empress Elizabeth in 1755 with the collaboration of the great encyclopaedist Lomonossov; in the pretty courtyards stand statues of Herzen and Ogarev. One side of the buildings faces a street which is also named after Herzen.

On the other end of this vast square, facing the Riding School, is the colossal Moskva Hotel, another example of Stalinite architecture in massive red granite and white marble, fourteen storeys high, containing many restaurants, hundreds of rooms and one basement exit that leads directly into the Moscow Underground. All along the longest side of Manège Square, facing the National Hotel, are delightful gardens under the crenellated red brick walls of the Kremlin, beyond which the bubble-like gilded domes of the churches inside the fortress can be seen.

A few steps away from Manège Square is the Bolshoi Theatre, another classical Greek edifice standing in Sverdlov Square, and where on my second visit to Moscow I was to see the Bolshoi Ballet performing *Giselle*. Also on this square are a number of other theatres, the enchanting Children's Theatre and the Maly Theatre, where traditional European tragedies and comedies are performed. Outside is a statue of the playwright Ostrovsky, some of whose plays were first performed at this theatre. Here too is the Metropol Hotel, with its fantastic, antiquated Arabian Nights dining-room, all palms and fountains and plush. Service here is by waiters only, and is somewhat better, I found, than at most Moscow or Leningrad hotels, though still erratic.

In Russian the word for 'red' (*krasnaya*) also means 'beautiful'. But I do not think Red Square is a beautiful square: to my mind the two most beautiful squares in Moscow are the Nogina Square, with its exquisite Church of Our Lady of Georgia, and Mayakovsky Square, with its splendid vistas of boulevards and, at its centre, the heroic and very impressive statue of the poet Mayakovsky.

The huge open space of Red Square is the most peculiar architectural mixture I have ever seen. It is a sort of sloping sea of cobbles, at the down-dipping end of which, like some phantasmagoric lighthouse, stands the grotesque Cathedral of St Basil, with its odd turnip-shaped domes at various heights, each decorated and coloured in a different fashion. The total effect is pretty but slightly absurd. As a building, it looks as crude as a stage-set for the Gingerbread House in *Hansel and Gretel*. It is garish and eccentric and exotic, but without a trace of true beauty or proportion. I am not surprised that the State has made it into a museum. GUM Department Store: pseudo-Haussmann.

Lenin's Tomb, in the centre of the sea, sheltered by the abrupt red-brick cliffs of the Kremlin walls, is stylistically the complete opposite of St Basil's. It is 'modernistic'. The Mausoleum is a set of low oblong blocks of shiny dark pink marble laid on top of one another in the form of steps, and it is so utterly featureless and dull that on my first visit to Red Square I failed to notice it. (It was a Sunday and the famous day-long queue winding round the square to view Lenin in aspic was missing.)

Two Red Army soldiers were standing absolutely motionless at either side of the door leading to the holy of holies where Lenin lies embalmed more or less for eternity. After reading Robert Payne's monumental and fascinating *Life and Death of Lenin* I developed a respectful affection for Vladimir Ilyich, one of the greatest human tyrants of all time. But I had no desire to see his embalmed body, so gruesomely dead, that body that is the heart of all modern Russia.

Nevertheless on another occasion I steeled myself to go into the Mausoleum and take a look. I had often read that if a foreign tourist presents himself at the front of the endless queue to see Lenin, he is at once invited to enter the Mausoleum without having to wait for hours in the shuffling queue. I duly presented myself at the front of the queue, but was indignantly pushed aside by outraged peasants and escorted to the end of the queue by a Red Army soldier, who gave me a very strict salute and did not smile. I felt as if I had provoked an international incident.

After about three hours I entered the Mausoleum. I went down a porphyry staircase into the distinctly chilly vault where I saw Lenin's face and hands—all that is visible of him—lying in a brilliantly lit glass box. I was not allowed to stop and take a good look, for the crowd has to be kept moving all the time. But at once, when I saw that face, I felt certain that it was a wax dummy. Only if I were allowed to touch the actual corpse would I be convinced that it was really Lenin.

On coming out of the Mausoleum I saw the tribunes where the Soviet leaders stand to welcome cosmonauts and popular parades on 1st May and 7th November. Here too were the famous tombs. I was particularly interested to see that of John Reed, whose *Ten Days that Shook the World* I have always much admired. This American Communist died in Russia in 1920, and his resting place is marked by a simple slab of granite.

Behind these collective graves of the revolutionary pantheon is a columbarium containing the ashes of many great Russians; these individual tombs are each surmounted by a commemorative bust in bronze. Here lie such famous names as Frunze, Sverdlov, Dzerzhinsky, Kirov, Ordzhonikidze, Kalinin, Zhdanov, and—Joseph Vissarionovich Dzhugashvily, commonly known as Stalin, who in October 1961 was suddenly removed from his place next to Lenin in the Mausoleum and laid here under a plain flagstone bearing his name and the dates 1879–1953. Other urns, set into the brick wall, contain the remains of such distinguished men as Lunacharsky, Gorky and Vishinsky. The latest arrival in the wall of the Kremlin is the pioneer cosmonaut, Yuri Gagarin. The ironic disaster of his death equals the tragedy of that of his fellow cosmonaut, Komarov, whose ashes also are in the wall. Eventually Gagarin and Komarov will be joined by all the other Soviet space heroes.

3
CONTRASTS IN THE CAPITAL

As MODERN cities go Moscow is fairly small: on 1st January 1967 its population was given as only 6,507,000. At the same time the Central Statistical Board of the U.S.S.R. reported that the entire population of Russia was 234,401,000. They are both curiously round figures, and one wonders exactly how they were arrived at. It is a fact that the Russian birth-rate has been steadily declining, and predictions that the population figure for the entire republic would exceed 300 million by the end of the century would now seem improbable. The decline in the birth-rate is a consequence of increasing urbanization and a higher living standard, and it is a pattern that can be seen all over Europe, though not in Asia, where every country excepting Japan—where the birth-rate is also declining sharply—is suffering from a population explosion.

The Soviet Government is now urging the people, through ceaseless propaganda in the press and other mass media, to have large families. However, if one wants to take a girl to one's hotel room in Moscow or Leningrad, the difficulties are almost insuperable. Girls don't like to be seen with foreigners in the first place. Then one has somehow to smuggle them past the Medusa squatting behind her desk of keys in the corridor of every floor in the hotel. Officially 'visitors' to hotel rooms are supposed to leave before 11 p.m. But at any hour of the day, if one is entertaining a friend, a chamber maid will always find some pretext to enter the room to find out if any hanky-panky is going on. It is most disturbing. It is a relic of puritanical Stalinism, I suppose, though by nature the Russians seem to be disapproving and anti-joy.

In my wanderings round Red Square, or after trying vainly to do some shopping in the woefully hot and antiquated GUM Departmental Store, I would take a quiet stroll along the pleasant quaysides of the Moskva River, from which unusual glimpses of St Basil's and the Kremlin can be obtained. From here I was also able to gaze upon the almost completed Rossia Hotel, the largest in Europe. (It is now open to the public.) It has accommodation for 6,000 guests and cost, it is said, over $100 million. The Rossia has 3,000 rooms, all wired for sound, and each with a bathroom. There are two cinemas, a swimming-pool on the roof, a 3,000-seat auditorium for conferences and concerts and several restaurants. The hotel is intended mainly to house delegates to the various Soviet Congresses, but tourists and foreign business men may be able to stay here during slack periods. As at all Soviet hotels, the room charges are high for foreigners—between seventy shillings and ten pounds a night, without meals.

There is a twenty-three storey tower on top of the twelve-storey west wing, containing four-room luxury apartments for distinguished artists and citizens. But what Moscow engineers claim is the highest television tower in the world stands in the suburb of Ostankino in the northern part of the city, a suburb more famous for the eighteenth-century Ostankino Palace of the Sheremetyev family, built by serf labour in classical Russian stucco-moulded style. It is a most luxurious place, and houses the Serf Museum and a beautiful little theatre. Near by is an exquisite Russian baroque building, the Church of the Trinity, all cupolas and tented belfries, with a free-standing steeple.

From the banks of the Moskva River, as well as from the heights of the new Moscow University overlooking the river and the city, I could appreciate very well the strange mingling of traditional and modern architecture. Moscow's skyscrapers have often been compared to wedding-cakes, and there is some truth in the comparison. They are immensely solid and prosaic, however, and have a curiously outmoded look. As I was trying to think what they reminded me of, I recalled the Twentyish skyscraper that illustrates the *New Yorker* magazine's 'Talk of the Town' column. I presume that these Moscow skyscrapers were modelled on already old-fashioned American structures. The Russians are feverishly anxious to outdo the U.S.A. in everything from space exploration to big business, and are almost succeeding in doing so, but in architecture they are way behind the times. Krushchev, reacting against Stalin's grandiose but comic monumentality, concentrated on putting up functional, utilitarian apartment blocks for the workers. The city is therefore both monumental and drab: its silent inhabitants look completely lost in it. More stadiums, parks, pools and lakes are planned in order to relieve the monotony of these dreary Moscow suburbs: but those squat, identical apartment blocks will remain, an image of unimaginative officialdom.

This drab utilitarianism does not extend to the Moscow Underground, which is truly one of the marvels of Moscow and indeed of the entire modern world. It was Nikita Krushchev himself who in 1935 supervised the construction of the first seven miles of the Moscow Underground, called the Metro, in accordance with Stalin's grandiose plans. Today one of the sights of Moscow is the sumptuousness of these Metro stations. They are spotlessly clean, spacious, quiet places, even at rush hours. The long, steep escalators move with great swiftness, and the walls are not disfigured by advertisements. Each station is an architectural marvel, both inside and out. Some of them have entrances like Greek temples or Roman forums. Each one is in a different style. The interiors are well but softly lighted with indirect lighting and shimmering chandeliers. Everywhere there are statues and paintings, as well as severe but lovely decorations of stainless steel, marble, majolica tiles, crystal lamp fittings. The floors are tiled with marble and mosaic. In some there are fountains. There is a feeling of great care and thought devoted to every detail. An army of cleaners is required, and they do their work invisibly and well, for there is not a speck of dust, no grease, no litter, no vending-machines, no noise, no sweat, no crush. I noted the absolute quietness of passengers between the far-apart stops, and the cool tranquillity of the platforms' colonnades, arcades and cloisters. A sense of reverence and security pervades one's mind in the Moscow Underground. Its stations are the new cathedrals of Soviet Russia. It is a great artistic as well as scientific achievement.

Art in Russia does not always enjoy such prosperity. In the field of music the Moscow Philharmonic Orchestra under its brilliant conductor Kyril Kondrashin and the Leningrad Philharmonic are great orchestras, and David and Igor Oistrakh are among the world's finest violinists. But there seems to be little new music of much interest coming out of Russia today apart from the pleasant compositions of Yuri Sviridov and the epic symphonies of Shostakovitch. The latter's opera, *A Macbeth of Mtsensk*, was banned by Stalin, who said it was too noisy and too 'formalistic'—this is the favourite word of Soviet art tyrants and Philistines. Incidentally this opera has now been made into a Soviet film, *Katerina Ismailova*, directed by Mikhail Chapiro. It was actually picked as the official Soviet entry in the 1967 Cannes International Film Festival. But Russia is still far behind the times in its appreciation of modern music: it was only recently that Webern (*Six Orchestral Pieces*) was given a hearing in Moscow, a performance that created much excitement.

The literary and political tribulations of Boris Pasternak and other Soviet poets and writers like Valery Tarsis, Mikhail Zoschenko and Anna Akhmatova are too well known already to merit discussion here. I should just like to quote from Robert Payne's interesting biography, *The Three Worlds of Boris Pasternak*, the following wry statement by the poet: 'I am a white cormorant. As everyone knows, there are only black cormorants.'

Though I have some doubts about the ultimate value to literature of the work of younger poets like Evtuschenko and Voznesensky, the former of whom often seems to be under some official cloud, I cannot see how they could do any better, given the circumstances under which they have to work. I made several requests to meet young poets and artists, but these were always denied me. They seem to live apart, in a world of their own, walking the difficult tightrope stretched between official approval of the Union of Soviet Writers and individualistic, unofficial freedom of self-expression. How can a poet create good work in such a climate? There is no encouragement to experiment or to express an unconventional point of view: poets who do so are simply not published and cannot get a hearing. Poets are often compelled, as they are in all countries, to descend to journalism or translation, and though the quality of Pasternak's translation is beyond doubt, one wonders why it should have been necessary for a writer of his calibre to have to support himself in this way. In the 'free world', as it is so hypocritically called, writers are accustomed to having to do hack work. One would have thought that in the 'ideal world' of the Soviet Union things would be different. A recent prose essay by Andrei Voznesensky on the ballerina Plisetskaya, which was published in translation in the *New York Review of Books*, was an extremely feeble piece of hack work, without originality or sensitivity.

In January 1967 an 'underground' poetry reading of highly experimental poems by an obscure and unconventional poet Dmitri Sukharevsky was suddenly banned by the authorities. It had been planned to hold the reading as a kind of protest following a showing of banned abstract paintings. But both the poems and the paintings had been viciously attacked as being 'formalistic'. At an extraordinary meeting of the Union of Soviet Artists held to plan artists' participation in the 1967 celebrations of the fiftieth year of Soviet power, the chairman of the Union, 'official' sculptor Yekaterina Belashova, asserted that young Soviet artists were devoting too much time and energy to empty 'formalistic' exercises.

The cancellation of the 'underground' poetry reading coincided with a fresh outburst of anti-nonconformist activity on the part of cultural officialdom, during which three water-colours by the Soviet *émigré* painter Marc Chagall were removed without explanation from an exhibition in the Tretyakov Art Gallery, Moscow's great collection of Russian painting. It has the world's finest assembly of icons from the seventeenth and eighteenth centuries, and others of extreme beauty, like 'Our Lady of Vladimir' from the twelfth century, 'The Annunciation', late fourteenth century and a superb 'Saint George and the Dragon' from the late fifteenth century. The gallery contains acres of paintings on historical and official subjects; most of these are not worth looking at, but there are good portraits by Kramskoy ('Portrait of Tolstoy') and Repin ('Portrait of Mussorgsky'). Repin is considered to be the greatest Russian nineteenth-century painter, and his disciple Serov is well represented here by some delightful studies in the French Impressionist style.

But the thing I really wanted to see at the Tretyakov Gallery was its famous collection of suppressed 'decadent' art, including the works of Chagall, Kandinsky, Larionov, Goncharova and many others. One has to obtain special permission from the cultural authorities in order to view these works. I was unable to obtain this special authorization. It is said that many of these 'banned' works may eventually be exhibited in the New Tretyakov Gallery which is to be opened near Gorky Park, but with the present intolerant temper of Russian cultural authorities, this does not seem very likely.

In Françoise Gilot's book, *Life with Picasso*, I found a number of interesting remarks by the artist on the defence of culture and the freedom of the artist. Picasso said:

> One *can* defend culture in a broad, general sense, if you mean by that the heritage of the past; but the right to free expression is something one seizes, not something one is given.... Only the Russians are naïve enough to think that an artist can fit into society. That's because they don't know what an artist is. What can the state do with the real artists, the seers? Rimbaud in Russia is unthinkable. Even Mayakovsky committed suicide. There is absolute opposition between the creator and the state....

This last phrase is true of course not only of Russia, but of every country. Poets are an impediment, they destroy the neatness of bureaucratic control, they disrupt preconceived ideas about art, patriotism, war and society. In England, for example, there is just the same kind of battle between the creator and the state in the battles waged by writers and artists with the new Ministry of Education and Science, with the Inland Revenue Department, which until recently taxed creative writers most unjustly, with the Arts Council and with the much-hated, much-feared, authoritarian and Philistine British Council.

Picasso goes on to say:

> So there's only one tactic for the state—kill the seers... there wouldn't be such a thing as a seer if there weren't a state trying to suppress him. It's only at that moment, under that pressure, that he becomes one. People reach the status of artist only after crossing the maximum number of barriers. So the arts should be *dis*couraged, not *en*couraged.

This ironical reversal at the end of Picasso's speech is of course intended half humorously, half seriously.

A similar attitude appears in Evgeny Evtushenko's *A Precocious Autobiography*, a most likable work. He tells us amusingly how he tried hard to become an 'official' poet, writing poems about football, volleyball, basketball, boxing, climbing, rowing and skating, as well as poems for special occasions like New Year's Day, May Day, Railwaymen's Day, Tank Corps Day and so on. He says:

> 'This form of occasional journalism in verse was very common in our country and unfortunately survives even today....'

In one of these 'official' poems which appeared in the paper *Trud* he was criticized because it did not contain any references to Stalin. Eventually, whenever he wrote a poem, the editor of the paper would automatically write in a few lines in praise of Stalin, something which Evtushenko accepted with indifference. But when his first book of poems appeared he saw their emptiness. This book, *The Prospectors of the Future*, appeared in 1952 and was well reviewed because the poems contained dutiful sentiments about Stalin. But when the poet saw his book on sale in the bookshops, he was overcome by disgust, and threw the money he had received for the volume into the Moskva River. (I am not altogether ready to believe the story of this melodramatic gesture.)

Later, Evtushenko writes about poets he admired: Vanshenkin, Vinokurov, and of distinguished poets in concentration camps—Zabolotsky and Smelyakov. The young poet Mandel had been deported for openly writing and reciting in public verses against Stalin and his regime. The flabbergasted authorities arrested him and then declared him insane. He speaks also of such writers as Leonid Martinov, Pasternak and Anna Akhmatova, Tvardovsky and Boris Slutsky.

From these accounts one realizes what a bitter battle any poet of sincerity must fight against the state.

I had heard that young Russian poets frequently gave impromptu poetry recitals from the plinth of the giant statue of Mayakovsky in Mayakovsky Square. Evtushenko and Voznesensky were sometimes to be heard there I was told. I went there every day on every visit I paid to Moscow, but never saw any sign of a poet or a poetry reading. So one evening I decided to hold my own poetry reading. In the summer twilight I got up on the high plinth with some difficulty and began declaiming, with oratorical gestures, some of my poems against war, and, in a more subdued style, a number of lyrics on Japanese subjects. I spoke for about half an hour, but no one took the slightest notice of me. Finally a policeman came along and demanded to know what I was doing, and ordered me to stop it at once. He helped me to get down from the pedestal and escorted me back to the nearby Minsk Hotel, where he checked my papers and advised me to go to bed. He must have thought I was drunk.

I got the impression that Russians, particularly Russian youths, are bored with politics and politicians. What they all want is what people want all over the world, a better life, freedom of movement, liberty of thought and expression, absence of tyranny. There are always some people, even in Russia, who attempt to break away from the stifling conformity of the modern police state. As I have said before, Soviet waiters and waitresses are abominably rude, but in a sense this rudeness is refreshing as an expression of individualism: to use a now outmoded phrase, they are showing signs of 'bourgeois ideology' in their summary treatment of their cowering customers.

Young people have a hunger for foreign things—exotic clothes, French movies, American cars. The cars of foreign tourists in the car park outside the Astoria Hotel in Leningrad were always surrounded by admiring youths. And I have commented on the yearning for chewing-gum, ball-point pens, cigarette lighters and so on. The more daring of Russian young people could sometimes be seen dancing a restrained twist on the dance floor of the Minsk Hotel dining-room. Officials were shocked to discover a recording studio in Gorky Street, a few steps from the Kremlin, in which certain youths had been learning and teaching rock 'n roll, the jerk, the frug, the swim and other 'decadent dances'. *Komsomol Moskovskaya* reported that this place, which it called 'a Temple of the Twist', was officially a studio where people came 'to record declarations of wholesome love or folk music'. The Komsomol newspaper added that it had been operating for nine years.

During my last visit to Moscow a new jazz restaurant was opened in the Slavyansky Bazaar or *Slavibaẓaa* which was formerly a luxurious Tsarist restaurant. The swing band wears golden jackets and long hair and the young customers dance the shag and jitterbug and occasionally twist. Though this abode of bourgeois luxury was closed down after the Revolution, the *décor* is still outrageously imperial, with high-arched ceilings, crystal chandeliers and elaborate table decorations. It is the most expensive place in Moscow, and the young people have to save up for months in order to go there and enjoy bourgeois decadence. A meal here takes at least three hours to order, consume and pay for.

Probably the quickest meal service in Moscow is at the new air-line terminal restaurant on Leningradsky Prospekt, where one is served by girls in air hostess uniforms whose blue skirts are about two inches above the knee, an unprecedented height in today's Russia. This restaurant is fairly cheap, and one can get in and out within forty-five minutes, a record for Russia. The food at both these restaurants is standardized Russian, not very interesting apart from the kebab, the cold mixed meat dishes, the Uzbekistan barbecues and Georgian garlic-flavoured chicken. But most of the items are nearly always 'off' on these establishments' gigantic menus.

4
MOSCOW MORNINGS AND MOSCOW NIGHTS

ONE of the much vaunted tourist attractions of Moscow is its theatres. I had been so disappointed and disillusioned by Russian life that I was now particularly eager to reverse my initial impressions by visits to the Bolshoi ballet and opera, to the Obratsov Puppet Theatre and houses like the Maly and the Stanislavsky, presenting classical and modern European and Russian drama. Such visits, I was sure, would change my whole outlook on Russia and the Russians.

On the night I arrived at the Hotel Minsk I went to the service bureau which one finds in the lobby of all Russian hotels. This bureau is supposed to cater to the needs of foreign tourists. I went to the theatre reservations desk and asked to be given tickets for performances held on the three nights of this my first visit to Moscow. I was quite willing to see anything, I explained.

The response of the bored young woman at the desk was deeply discouraging.

'No tickets for anything,' she snapped.

I was incredulous.

'But the main reason I am visiting Moscow is to see the theatre,' I said. She merely gave the Russian shrug.

'Where can I see some performances?' I persisted.

'Gorky Park of Culture and Rest,' she growled. She made the awkward name sound like a curse.

'What kind of performances?' I asked.

'Open-air concert parties, folk-singing, displays of workers' crafts,' was all I could get out of her. It was not exactly what I had in mind. Still, I felt it was better than nothing, and asked her how to get to Gorky Park.

'Anyone will tell you,' she snapped. 'Take a bus.'

'Will you try to get me a ticket for something tomorrow night?' I asked.

'I already told you, no tickets for anything.'

I then hit on a method of dealing with such women which I found very effective. I burst into tears. I sat there looking helpless and lost. I took out my Parker pen and offered it to her as a bribe. She was about to pocket it when she saw the other women assistants in the service bureau watching, and hastily withdrew her hand.

'What shall I *do*?' I wept, wiping my eyes. I have this very great talent for being able to turn on the waterworks at an instant's notice. It was obviously, I noted through my tears, disconcerting the stony-faced young woman before me.

'If I do not see the Bolshoi while I am in Moscow I shall kill myself!' I declared passionately with a dramatic gesture. I could see she was beginning to waver.

'Come back tomorrow at five,' she muttered, piercing me with her steely blue eyes. 'And don't be late.'

Mopping up my tears and holding my scented handkerchief tragically to my lips, I tottered away from her desk, hearing her mutter behind my back a contemptuous remark which must have meant 'decadent bourgeois weakling'.

I went to Gorky Park, which lies between the Moskva River and Lenin Avenue. It is a fantastic place. The entrance is unmistakable: an immense triumphal arch with a massive architrave on which are displayed the emblems of the Communist Party. It was packed with strollers out for a leisurely evening under the lantern-hung trees, pergolas, bowers and arcades. On the Pushkin Embankment was a wide promenade along the river, where ferry-boats were continually bringing fresh visitors. There were exhibitions of agricultural machinery and folk-art, dance halls, restaurants, beer halls, cinemas, libraries and pavilions for chess-players. There was also a huge open-air theatre with seats for twelve thousand people, where the Bolshoi ballet sometimes performs in summer time. But on that evening there was only some dull provincial folk-song chorus group. I thought how pleasant it must be here in winter, when the avenues are flooded with water to make them into outdoor skating rinks.

Indeed the winter is a festive time in Moscow, and it is the best period to enjoy the lively arts. Moscow and Leningrad in summer are off-seasons, artistically speaking. If one is a member of a delegation or an officially sponsored travel group, one is automatically given seats at the ballet and the opera and the Obratsov Puppet Theatre. But single travellers like myself are frowned upon, and Russia does everything it can to discourage such travel. Groups can be guided and controlled and brain-washed: strong-minded individuals are much more difficult to regiment. Later on I found that by going to one of the kiosks selling theatre tickets in the streets I was always able to get a ticket for some kind of show or concert, especially if I offered the lady ticket-seller—usually a grim, middle-aged harpy—a monetary gift or a ball-point pen or a packet of American cigarettes. There are also ticket scalpers outside all the big Moscow and Leningrad theatres. They sidle up to one and ask if one has a ticket for sale. If not, they offer one for the evening's performance at about twenty times the original cost: prices in Russian theatres are quite low, even for the best seats.

Next evening I presented myself at the theatre desk in the service bureau on the stroke of five. The woman did not even allow me to sit down. Without a word she produced a ticket for the Bolshoi opera, which was performing that evening in one of the theatres inside the Kremlin walls. This truly splendid theatre is housed in the immense modern Congress Building (*Dvoriets Siezdov*) which was inaugurated in October 1961 for the twenty-second Congress of the Communist Party. It is a structure of impressive functional purity, and so looks oddly out of place among the older buildings of the red-walled fortress. It looks like a huge lighted rectangle of glass and aluminium, its tall windows framed in slender white marble pylons. The 'theatre' is actually a large conference hall, one of the biggest in the world, and seating six thousand on the wide ground floor and in the galleries and side galleries. It is equipped with a vast stage, stereophonic sound and installations for simultaneous interpretation in twenty-nine languages. The stage is even wider than the Bolshoi's, and the orchestra pit can be raised or lowered by special lifting machinery. Banks of swiftly moving escalators take one up to the various floors and right on to the roof, where there is an enormous reception room laid with scores of well-appointed buffet tables. The walls of this hall are all glass, and afford spectacular views over the gilded tower tops and turnip-domes of the Kremlin's churches and palaces—the Terems Palace, the Tsarina's Golden Palace, the churches of the Redemption, the Resurrection and the Crucifixion. As one nibbles a self-served buffet supper and sips a glass of chilled punch, it is delightful to gaze through the immense double windows at those clusters of gilded onion-domes tinted bright orange by the setting sun: one had always gazed up at them from the ground, but now they are at eye level, a very revealing and extraordinary view of those remarkable structures. Indeed I think the Muscovites go to performances in this building in order to enjoy the views and the rich array of food and drink in the intervals as much as the performances themselves. I thought this Congress Building in the Kremlin was easily the most impressive piece of modern architecture I had ever seen in Russia, though I had also marvelled at the soaring rocket-shape of the 100-metre-high Cosmonauts' Memorial Tower in the Avenue of the Heroes in northern Moscow. It is made of titanium, and in front of it is a piece of quite good official statuary—most unusual in Russia—representing Konstantin Ziolkovsky, the Russian rocket pioneer. The Congress Building has the same feeling of urgency and adventurousness as the Cosmonauts' Memorial Tower. Certainly its escalators move at such a breath-taking speed that one sometimes feels one is about to be launched into orbit from the roof. Indeed at the top of each flight of the six-storey escalators one had to look pretty smart and hop off very quickly. There was some confusion at these turns because people simply couldn't keep up with the hectic pace of the escalator, and there was much stumbling, crowding and pushing. The escalators had the same swift, silent smoothness as those in the Metro.

I was rather disappointed by the opera and by the manner in which it was staged and performed. It was Mussorgsky's *Khovanshtchina*, and I found it an almost unmitigated bore. It is a long historical affair with undistinguished music. The sets and costumes were hardly any better than those of a provincial British Christmas pantomime. However, I enjoyed watching the lighting, which was done with great virtuosity, and the movement of crowd scenes, which was impeccably stage-managed. The programme was entirely in Russian, so I could follow nothing of the obviously very complex plot. I did not stay for the final act, but went up to the roof again for a final view of those incredible golden domes, then walked slowly back to my hotel, calling in on the way at the dear old-fashioned Metropol Hotel, one of the two hotels in Moscow which has a bar. (The other is the National.) The bar at the Metropol does not open until 9 p.m. It was long, bleak and empty except for one bartender. I ordered a Screwdriver, very badly made. I was given a straw to drink it through: in Russia these plastic straws are extremely thin, and one almost bursts a blood-vessel trying to draw on one. Only *one* straw is ever given of course: a second is always refused. To drink through *two* straws at the same time would be considered the ultimate in effete bourgeois luxuriousness. Curiously one seems to drink more quickly through these excessively thin straws, for once one starts sucking one can't stop. I suppose it is because the rate of the stream is the same as that of milk from the human breast; this takes us back to the bottle, and we all become babes in arms again.

When I paid for my drink with a dollar bill (only dollars are accepted in these two 'degenerate' bars, which are nearly always empty) the bartender insisted on giving me my change in Russian currency. I protested at this, saying that as I had paid him in dollars the least he could do was to give me change in American currency. But he refused. He said he had no American money to give for change. I offered him Polish currency instead, but this he looked at with contemptuous sneers and then pushed over my change in Russian currency.

I found this attitude in all the hotel shops where souvenirs, vodka and caviar are sold for dollars, and also in the one or two shops now opened outside the hotels where one can buy foreign goods. They never have American small change. This is because they are so anxious to get their hands on every dime and cent. It is said that the Russians use the metal alloys in American coins in their space programme.

Even in Japan, at the office of Intourist at the Japan Travel Bureau in Marunouchi, Toshiro Ito, who was in charge of my travel arrangements to the U.S.S.R., had insisted that I should pay part of the fare in dollars. As I was allowed, by law, to buy only $500 in travellers' cheques with my yen currency, I did not wish to spend half of this on my fare. I foolishly and weakly paid over part of my fare in dollars, though I realize now that this was sheer extortion, and that I should have refused absolutely to pay any dollars. It certainly ran me short of cash during my trip through Russia.

Russians are very anxious to obtain 'hard' currencies, especially dollars. But they look down their noses at Polish, Czech, Yugoslav, Hungarian, Bulgarian and other Iron Curtain currencies, in which they apparently have no faith at all. Yet another example of modern Russia's new bourgeois attitudes. For Russia, it is only the money of capitalist countries that seems to have any steady value. The rest is rubbish.

I found the same difficulty on my second visit to Moscow, when I was staying at the Hotel Ukraina. Here the large 'Beriozka' souvenir shops had some very desirable things, particularly fur hats and embroidered shirts, caviar and various excellent brands of vodka—Petrovskaya, Stolichnaya and my favourite Stolovaya, the strongest kind. They also had some beautiful articles in various shades of amber ranging from off white to deep brown. There was also a lot of trash—badges and trinkets and models of sputniks, rockets and the

Cosmonauts' Memorial—and objects of curious but dubious charm, like the crudely painted *matriushka* dolls, which screw open at the waist to reveal ever smaller *matriushka* inside. Some of these contain as many as six or seven diminishing dolls, all showing plain-faced, head-scarved Russian matrons. They do have a certain dignity, but none of the humour of Japanese *kokeshi*. A type of Japanese *kokeshi* produced at Kanazwa on the Japan Sea coast right opposite the shores of Russia does indeed look rather like the Russian *matriushka*, but the colours and design and the pretty wit of the features makes this Japanese doll far superior to any Russian one. I suppose that the Kanazawa *kokeshi*, with its pretty features peeping out of a headscarf, has been influenced by the Russian dolls.

In the 'Beriozka' shops in the arcades of the Hotel Ukraina I had to pay for all these things in dollars. But they never had change in American currency. I heard many customers complaining about this, and not just Americans either. A number of visitors on Iron Curtain country delegations who had somehow provided themselves with American dollars were particularly furious about having to accept Russian currency in change for this 'hard' money.

There were also counters selling things for roubles, and here I bought a number of pretty gauze silk scarves, to air mail to girl friends in England and Japan. The ones I sent to Japan reached their destinations safely, but those I dispatched to England never arrived. I think the nicest things I bought were an embroidered cap and two embroidered linen shirts from Uzbekistan and Kiev: these are indeed enchanting in their fine but naïve peasant decoration. I sometimes wear the shirts as nightshirts.

After that first visit to the Congress Building, I was offered a few other tickets: my crocodile tears had certainly done the trick! So I was able to go to the puppet theatre, which was showing a kind of science fiction satirical fantasy, extremely inventive and funny; and to the Bolshoi Theatre itself, to see *Giselle* in a superlative production, though not as fine as the one I was to see by the Kirov Ballet in Leningrad (and later in London). The Bolshoi Theatre is an extremely handsome building, both inside and out: the chandeliered interior, all gilt and crimson plush, is simply ravishingly pretty, and on a grand scale. Most of the audience was composed of foreigners, chiefly English, belonging to a British trade delegation, all very suburban and Wimbledonian in their upper middle-class pretensions. (At the Ukraina Hotel I received a number of mysterious telephone calls, one mysteriously from a Chinese prostitute and another from the Commercial Attaché of the British Embassy who apparently thought I was Sir Frank Hoskisson, leader of the British trade delegation. I pretended to be Sir Frank for a few moments, until the attaché began talking about some intimate matters, when I revealed my identity. 'And what are *you* doing in Moscow?' he demanded. 'Just passing through,' I retorted, and hung up on him. This episode showed me how easy it could be to have one's conversation monitored in Russia, particularly at the Hotel Ukraina, a vast complex of buildings at whose twelfth floor the lift never stops, for it is given over entirely to studios recording the telephone conversations of residents and the conversations they hold with friends; all the rooms are 'bugged'.)

I was in a side box in the first gallery of the Bolshoi. The chairs were small and it was rather cramped; I was crowded against three large young women, who were extremely nice to me. I often found that at the theatre, particularly at the Bolshoi, Russians are on their very best behaviour. The girls wept openly at the tragedy of *Giselle*. During the interval I went down to the luxurious basement buffet, where everyone was queueing for canapes, caviar and glasses of raspberry cordial or champagne. It was an evening of real wonder and enchantment. It helped to erase some of the most unpleasant memories of my days in Russia.

The only other time I had any really human contact with a Russian girl was at the Hotel Minsk. I had handed in my laundry to be washed. I was told it would take two, maybe three, days. One night I had gone to bed after midnight when there came a knock at the door. I was sleeping naked, and hastily draped myself in a sheet. When I opened the door, there was a pretty Russian chambermaid standing before me, smiling and saying something in Russian about my laundry. She wanted me to pay for it there and then! As I staggered round my room in my sheet, that kept slipping, trying to pick my clothes off the floor and find some roubles in my pockets, the chambermaid suddenly became convulsed with laughter. Had she caught a glimpse of my bare bottom? Nervously I adjusted my sheet, drawing it up tightly under my chin. This only increased her giggles. She ran along to the end of the corridor and brought the middle-aged gorgon from the key desk to have a look at me. They both began laughing helplessly and wiping their eyes. That moment remains in my mind as something very precious: a brief interlude of human feeling in an inhuman world. I joined in their laughter, and indeed tried to provoke it by adjusting my toga-like sheet in ever more ridiculous ways, until in the end I found myself performing a kind of strip-tease in the corridor, coyly revealing now a hairy ankle, now a dimpled knee, now a rosy backside. It was hilarious. But next morning, when I went to collect my glass of tea and lump of sugar from the samovar at the end of the corridor, the lady of the keys was as stony-faced as ever. Jokes and laughter are obviously severely rationed in her world.

I used to get up at dawn every morning to wander the streets of Moscow. This was easily the nicest time of the day. The streets were deserted except for women hosing them down with gallons and gallons of water. The pavements and roads would all be gleaming wet in the pale, pearly light of morning. I was impressed by this scrupulous cleanliness of the main streets of Moscow. I took some pictures of these cleaning operations, to the great disgust of one of the women cleaners, who stabbed her finger at my camera and shook her fist at me in outrage. Actually it was not the woman I had been photographing, but the reflections of the sky in the wet pavements that shone like mirrors. It was lovely to walk in the fresh, cool air of morning in the empty streets: what a relief it was not to see any Russians with their ungainly bodies and surly faces! Moscow is at its most beautiful when there are no people about; in this respect it is just the exact opposite of Japan, where a street devoid of people is a street devoid of beauty and grace. Without people, Japan would be nothing. Without people, Russia is finally something, a place of calm loveliness. Those early mornings are my best memories of my walks in Moscow.

I had a coupon entitling me to the services of a professional guide. After much grumbling, the girl in the service bureau at the Hotel Minsk arranged for me to go on a guided tour of Moscow by taxi. My guide was late. When he did turn up he was not a professional at all, but a university student whose mentality was of the dimmest. His English was utterly incomprehensible, and he knew very little about Moscow. I had seen enough of the Kremlin and Red Square, so I asked him to take me to some other places. Unfortunately he did not know any other places. I had to show him the way all the time, for I knew more about Moscow than he did. The taxi-driver held him in open contempt, and seemed very reluctant to take orders from him. I often noticed that taxi-drivers engaged by Intourist are surly and unhelpful: this one gave my guide absolutely no assistance. I was sitting in the back of the car, a battered Zim, while the guide sat in front with the driver. Russia is one of the countries, like Malaysia and Indonesia, where it is quite usual for the passenger to sit next to the driver in a taxi: I often saw single women sitting next to the driver.

I wanted to see the great Lenin Library near Manège Square, for I had heard that my works were well represented there, and that my books about Japan were so popular that they had had to be microfilmed. This information came to me from a British librarian who had been on a conducted tour. However, when we got to the Lenin Library, my guide discovered that we had to have a special permit to enter, so I was unable even to get a look at the catalogue.

Then I asked to be taken to the Pushkin Museum. The guide did not know where it was, but I pleaded with the driver to take us there, which he did, very unwillingly, saying he could not wait outside the museum longer than ten minutes. Ten minutes to see this wonderful collection of modern art! I made no comment, but went in quite decided to stay at least one hour. The guide tried to rush me through at express speed, and every time I stopped to look at a picture he would tap his foot impatiently and glance at his watch. Photography is permitted in this museum, and I wanted to take a number of pictures, but the guide assured me photography was not allowed.

'Then why are so many people taking pictures?' I asked.

'They have special permits from the police,' he replied.

I went on taking pictures, and no one tried to stop me. French painting is particularly well represented in the Pushkin Museum—Courbet and Manet, magnificent Monets of Nympheas, *Déjeuner sur l'herbe*, Houses of Parliament; Pissarro, Dégas, and the most lovely Signacs I have seen anywhere. The Corots of the early and middle periods are exquisite, and there are great works by Daubigny and Theodore Rousseau and a fine male head and shoulders by Géricault.

There is a large collection of Gauguins including a haunting self-portrait. Van Gogh is also well represented, most memorably for me by his frightening 'Prison Yard', a painting that seems to take on added significance in a police state. There are some curious Cézannes—a self-portrait, landscapes, clown and harlequin. For the first time I saw here the boldly beautiful ceramic plaque portraits by Léger. Almost the whole of Picasso's Blue Period is to be seen here. There is a marvellous Douanier Rousseau of a horse attacked by leopards.

Many of these great paintings I was to see later, and admire more at my leisure, in a huge exhibition of art from the Pushkin and Hermitage Museums held in Tokyo's Museum of Modern Art, including Picasso's

'Absinthe Drinker', 'La Dryade' and several cubist seated nudes. In order to see the Pushkin Museum properly, one should spend at least one day there. A snack bar serving champagne and caviar is in the basement.

My tour of the city ended at lunch time with a splendid view of the whole of Moscow seen from Lenin Heights, the high plateau on which stands the gigantic new University of Moscow: I have never seen a building so lacking in humanity. It suggested an enormous termitary of cement. I turned away from its pompous cliffs with relief to gaze out over the city, which was looking lovely in the summer sun that here and there caught the glittering gilt of some church's turnip-domes among bowers of green trees.

PART FOUR

A GRADUAL DEPARTURE

I

LOVELY LENINGRAD

I was to leave Moscow from the Riga station for Leningrad on the Red Arrow express sleeper which leaves every midnight. At my hotel I was told to be ready to meet an Intourist guide who would conduct me to the station by taxi at ten o'clock. It seemed rather early to leave on the fifteen-minute or so ride to the station. But I had learnt not to argue in the U.S.S.R. So I was in the lobby with my bags towards ten o'clock.

There was no Intourist guide in sight, so I sat down to wait. About eleven o'clock a large bedraggled party of foreign tourists arrived, looking weary and sad. It had taken them hours to get through the airport customs and immigration, as I was told by their leader, a very lively young American from Ohio. He was a professional courier, and warned me that as my Intourist guide had not turned up I had better make my own way to the station. I went outside and tried to hail a taxi, but at that time of night they are practically unobtainable in Moscow. Nor are there taxi ranks outside hotels. Late at night I have often had to make my way back to my hotel on foot.

Beginning to feel rather worried, I came back into the hotel, and found the weary band of tourists still stranded in the lobby while the endless registration proceedings went on. They were all moaning for baths, drinks, food, bed. One woman, who had broken her leg, was demanding to see a doctor, but no one took any notice of her.

I complained to one of the desk clerks that my Intourist taxi had not arrived, and would she please summon a taxi for me at once, or I would miss the Red Arrow. She shrugged. I went to one of the hall porters, and he was a little more sympathetic, though he implied that this was none of his business. He telephoned the lady in charge of the keys on the floor where I had been staying. Apparently she was responsible for getting me a taxi. This lady came panting down into the lobby in a great state of agitation. It transpired that my taxi had indeed arrived about ten o'clock, but without the Intourist guide whose services one automatically pays for when buying a train ticket. No one had thought of telling me that my taxi was waiting, and the driver had not bothered to come inside and call me: it was not his job. After waiting fifteen minutes he had left without telling anyone.

The lady of the keys berated the hall porters. The hall porters berated the lady of the keys. Then they all started berating me. Despite her ill temper, I could see that the lady of the keys was extremely upset; this mistake might cost her her job at the Minsk Hotel and bring her a severe rebuke from Intourist. Incensed, she ordered one of the hall porters to go out into the street and hail a taxi for me. By now it was a quarter to midnight. I knew how difficult it was to get a taxi at that time of night, and began to have serious doubts as to whether I should catch my train. If not, would my fare be refunded? I had no money to buy another ticket, and in any case it would not be my fault if I missed the train. The large party of tourists, still milling round the lobby, was obviously going to fill most of the vacant rooms. Could I find accommodation for the night if I were to miss the Red Arrow?

Everyone was in a stew, but I found myself to be quite indifferent. I no longer cared what happened to me in Russia. I had been through so many horrible experiences that my present predicament seemed without importance.

A taxi was found for me at seven minutes to midnight. The driver was given instructions to drive at top speed to the Riga station. The lady of the keys asked me if I had money to pay the taxi: the taxi fare is included in the price of the train ticket issued by Intourist. Once again, through the inefficiency of this tourist organization, I was to lose money. I leapt into the taxi and it sped away at an alarming speed. Fortunately there was very little traffic. We arrived at the station at just one minute to midnight. I flung a rouble note at the driver and sprinted to the train, which was just beginning to move off. A woman guard opened a door, pulled in my bags and dragged me inside. It was the last carriage on the train. My own seat was near the front, so I had to make my way through about a score of rocking carriages before I reached it.

The Red Arrow is a superb train. It was the first comfortable train ride I had in Russia. The two-berth compartment was luxuriously appointed, with a shower, toilet and wash-basin shared with the next-door compartment. A train girl brought round snacks, tea and cognac. Unfortunately I was sharing my compartment with an Englishman, someone from the B.B.C. who had an extremely heavy cold. He told me proudly about his experiences as a B.B.C. reporter in Moscow, how he had interviewed leading actors and writers and visited Zagorsk for the four hundredth anniversary celebrations. He had been covering the British Trade Fair in Moscow. He was very surprised when I told him I had come all the way from Nakhodka by train, and that I would be returning to Japan by that route in a few months' time. Then he spotted my name on my luggage, and at once fell silent. It is well known that I am on the B.B.C.'s 'black list' of unco-operative writers with dangerous pacifist beliefs. I am glad to say I did not catch his cold.

I took a Nembutal and slept about four hours. A pearly dawn broke over dark, flat, wooded landscape, its fields neatly scythed. About a year later, when I was reading two new and beautiful books about Russia, Konstantin Paustovsky's *In That Dawn* and Vladimir Soloukhin's *A Walk in Rural Russia*, I was reminded of the pastoral loveliness of the vast spaces of the Ukraine, Siberia and this region round Lake Ladoga. Vladimir Nabokov's *Speak Memory* is also replete with evocations of this utterly unique rural beauty, which is one of Russia's great links with its past: no revolution can ever change its enormous solitude and wide, tall skies.

We crossed a big river just past Novgorod, 'the cradle of the Russian nation', a city from that ideal Russian past that is almost fairy-like in its medieval perfection. In the ninth century the Viking chieftain Rurik, one of my own ancestors, set up his fortified camp at Novgorod (which means 'new town'). His warriors were called 'Rus' (meaning 'of the earth') and their settlement in Novgorod, at the invitation of the rebel Russian Slav peoples, was the beginning of the modern Russian state.

After we had passed this big river the landscape began to look increasingly Scandinavian. Haystacks became rectangular, with a pole at each corner supporting a rough wooden roof. The charming farmhouses were in log cabin style, with prettily painted windows. The mowers were out early, their scythes wet with light and sparkling like jets of water as they flashed through the long rich grasses and galaxies of wild flowers. There were also many old women strolling by the train embankment, pasturing cows on a leash. I saw a railside grave, adorned with flowers, a post with a red star on top.

The countryside was quite flat, and the railroad was dead straight. It is said that when this railway line was being constructed the Tsar simply took a ruler and drew a straight line between Moscow and Leningrad. He instructed his engineers to build the track following this line exactly, and they did. The four hundred kilometres are without a single curve.

When I reached Finland station I remembered how Lenin had arrived there from Zürich in a sealed train provided by the Germans on the night of 16th April 1917. The next day he announced his *April Theses*, calling for the overthrow of the 'bourgeois' provisional government and the transfer of all power to the Soviets.

I was met by an Intourist guide who conducted me to my hotel, the Astoria, a charming old building with large rooms and old-fashioned furniture. It is one of Russia's best hotels, and I enjoyed my stay there.

After my long night trip on the train I was longing for a bath and breakfast. But after handing in my passport at the reception desk I was told I should have to wait one hour before I could go to my room. I spent the time breakfasting in a little snack bar which is part of the large restaurant: here I enjoyed excellent coffee, cake, open sandwiches of compressed black sticky caviar on slabs of brown bread, an apple and champagne. The Astoria restaurant is quite good, with one of the best dance bands I ever heard in Russia playing in the evenings. But the service is woefully slow; lunch takes two hours, dinner three hours. And there are the usual large gaps in the enormous menu.

The waiters in the Astoria Hotel, as well as those in most Russian hotels, wore a special kind of old-fashioned bow tie stuck with an artificial pearl pin, whose 'wings' were tucked away under the points of the shirt collar. This kind of tie seemed to be the unofficial badge of waiters in Russia, though I did see it worn by several young men who were not waiters. I found some examples of this neckwear in a men's haberdashery on the Nevsky Prospekt, Leningrad's main shopping street. They were available in only two colours, dark red and dark green, ready-made, and fastened round the neck, under the shirt collar, with a length of elastic. When I reached England I picked up Tom Wolfe's extremely amusing and hilariously well-written book about pop-art culture, *The Kandy-Koloured Tangerine-Flake Streamline Baby*, and found a reference to this quaint kind of necktie in a scintillating essay on one of my heroes, Cassius Clay or Muhammad

Ali, as I should more properly call him. The essay contains this phrase:

> The management, a lot of guys in tuxedos with the kind of Hollywood black ties that tuck under the collars and are adorned with little pearl stickpins and such devices . . .

The reference is to the management of a dance café in New York called the Metropole Café. It was odd to find these 'Hollywood' ties in Russia. In England I found they were very popular with both mods and rockers. I bought a couple, but found they did not wear well: they were badly made, soon looked crumpled, and the poor quality Russian elastic soon lost its snap. In another essay Tom Wolfe refers to those rubber sandals from Japan which one now sees all over the world: he calls them 'rubber Zorrie sandals'. The name 'Zorrie' is presumably derived from the Japanese name for such traditional-style sandals made of straw or fine-woven rush—*zori*. But I never saw anyone wearing these sandals in Russia. Indeed I never saw anyone with bare feet in Russia, except on the beaches. Perhaps Japanese rubber 'Zorries' are considered a symbol of bourgeois capitalist decadence. I find them eminently practical, and not as expensive as conventional sandals, but then I regard myself as a typical product of Western bourgeois decadence.

After breakfast I was finally allowed to go up to my room in a creaking, old-fashioned lift lined with mirrors; it had a plush-covered bench and an ancient electric fan that blew one's hair all over the place. There was a small rack of well-thumbed picture magazines with which one could beguile the time as one ascended from the ground floor to the sixth floor—a journey that took at least ten minutes.

My room was large and comfortable, full of solid old-style furnishings. There was no bath, but a wash-basin (no hot water and, of course, no plug). I had to go down to a dank, echoing cavern at the end of the corridor where the bathroom and the communal toilets were situated.

The first thing I did in my room at the Astoria was to twiddle the little wheel in the base of the telephone and to disconnect the tiny radio. There was a suspicious-looking ventilator up in the wall above my bed, and at this I shouted obscene greetings night and morning. I received three telephone calls while at the Astoria—all from girls offering their services. I always refused, and then they would spit out some angry curse at me and bang down the receiver. I met a nice Japanese girl in Leningrad, and I invited her up to my room. She accepted my invitation, which was quite innocent: I merely wanted to show her some pictures I had taken in the small ancient town of Hagi, on the Japan Sea coast, from which she hailed. But we were stopped in the corridor by the lady keeping the keys: she said it was improper for me to take a foreign lady into my room. However, later I took a Russian girl to my room without comment.

I arranged my guided tour of Leningrad at the service bureau in the lobby of the Astoria, where I found the assistants much kinder and more helpful than in Moscow. Without asking, I was offered tickets for the Kirov ballet at the exquisite little theatre on Theatre Square called officially the Academic Theatre of Opera and Dance, but which everyone calls simply the Kirov. Formerly the Marinsky Theatre, it was first used as the Tsar's circus. I was also given tickets to concerts at the National Conservatory of Leningrad, which stands just opposite the Kirov Theatre.

My guide to Leningrad was a pleasant and well-informed young man who was acting in this capacity during his holidays from a technical college. He was extremely kind and attentive, and seemed so unusually open-minded about everything that I ventured to ask him questions I would never dream of addressing to most Russians.

'Are there many male and female prostitutes in Leningrad?' I asked.

'No,' he answered simply, but with a telltale blush.

'Do you go to church?'

'No.' The blush was replaced by a look of indifference.

'Do you like foreign cigarettes?' I asked, offering him a packet of Japanese 'Peace' and 'Hope' cigarettes.

His eyes lit up at the sight of these. He was particularly impressed by the beautiful design of a dove of peace on the 'Peace' packet. He accepted them with a smile and a handshake.

'We Russians are for peace,' he declared.

'So am I,' I told him, showing him my C.N.D. badge, of whose significance he was not aware until I explained it to him. Indeed no one in Russia knew what the symbol on the badge referred to.

'Ah! Bertrand Russell!' he beamed. 'A great man! We admire him very much in Russia.'

I agreed with him entirely about Bertrand Russell. Then he asked me:

'Have you any American jazz records?'

As it happened I had some long-playing records featuring my favourite American singer, Anita O'Day, and a new disc by Eric Dolphy as well as Sonny Rollins's new 'Alfie' recording. I could not bring myself to part with Anita, but promised to let him have the Eric Dolphy and the Sonny Rollins when we got back to the hotel.

Right outside the Astoria is a truly magnificent example of church architecture, St Isaac's Cathedral, with its immense dome and colonnaded rotunda. Most of these huge Olonets granite columns still bear scars of the war-time bombardments when the greater part of Leningrad was reduced to rubble. It is a noble structure in the old Imperial Russian style of monumental grandeur. The tremendous bronze doors open to reveal a sumptuously decorated interior of polychrome marble, lapis lazuli and malachite. I went up into the dome—where photography is forbidden—and enjoyed a superb bird's-eye view of Leningrad and the surrounding countryside. I could see as far as Kronstadt, a port situated on the island of Kotlin in the Gulf of Finland, at the extreme tip of which stands Leningrad. The island and the town of Kronstadt form the strongest naval base in the Baltic, and the Soviet Baltic fleet anchors here, which is perhaps one of the reasons why photography is not permitted from the dome of St Isaac's. Kronstadt has been immortalized in the great Russian films about the cruiser *Aurora* and the sailors' revolutionary mutinies. Foreign visitors are not allowed in Kronstadt, and even Russians themselves still have to obtain a special permit to go there. I often watched the boat for Kronstadt leaving Leningrad from the Makarov Quay, near the old Stock Exchange, and wondered if I should ever be able to go there: it is quite possible that regulations may be relaxed in the future.

The whole of the vast Neva delta lay spread before my eyes. I was conscious of the severely geometrical layout of Leningrad. I found myself looking directly down at two main squares, the Decembrists' and St Isaac's, and on the straight, broad streets, including the Nevsky Prospekt, converging on the Admiralty building with its fine pillared tower topped by a slender golden spire with a weather-vane in the shape of a ship, just like the one on the town hall at South Shields. The façade is all columns and pedestals and nymphs and fountains. The building was begun by Peter the Great in 1704, but its present remodelled appearance dates from the early nineteenth century. Its style seems to have influenced the colossal 'wedding-cake' skyscrapers of the Stalin era in Moscow.

I could see part of another delightful spot in central Leningrad, the pretty little Workers' Garden ornamented with statues of writers and poets—Yukovsky, Gogol, Lermontov—and the composer Glinka and the explorer Pergevalsky. Here I often used to stroll among the fountains on those bright sunny summer afternoons, or sit reading Proust on the benches, while the Neva sparkled beyond the trees, over which rose the glittering gold steeple of the Admiralty. I began to feel that Leningrad was an enchanted city.

My guide and I visited all the main points in Leningrad. On the Nevsky Prospekt there are a number of fascinating buildings, including one on the corner of Gogol Street which has been modelled on the Palace of the Doges in Venice and was originally intended to be a bank. It now houses state co-operatives.

An interesting old house was pointed out to me by my guide on the section of the Prospekt between Herzen Street and the Moika. It was built on the site of the former wooden palace of the Empress Elizabeth, daughter of Peter the Great. Here the French sculptor Falconet had a studio, in which he cast the statue of Peter the Great that dominates Decembrists' Square near the Neva. The statue is an equestrian one, with Peter astride a war-horse trampling on a huge snake. It is interesting to see how the horse, rearing magnificently on its hind legs, is given strength and balance by making the great sweeping tail hang down right to the plinth, a block of Lacta granite weighing thousands of tons. The statue was commissioned by Catherine II in honour of Peter the Great, and it was this monument that Pushkin celebrated in his long poem 'The Bronze Horseman', a poem that is also a celebration of the city of Leningrad itself:

> ... the young city, the ornament and marvel of the northern climes, rose, resplendent and stately, from the dark forests and the swamps. Where once the Finnish fisherman, Nature's wretched stepson, alone on the low-lying banks, cast his ancient net into unknown waters, now along the banks astir with life tall and graceful palaces and towers cluster; ships from all the ends of the earth hasten in throngs to the rich quays; the Neva has clothed herself in granite; bridges hang above the waters; her islands have become covered with dark-green gardens; ... and old Moscow has paled before the younger capital, like a dowager clad in purple before a new empress.
>
> I love you, Peter's creation, I love your severe, graceful appearance, the Neva's majestic current, the granite of her banks, the tracery of your cast-iron railings, the transparent twilight, the moonless gleam of your still nights, when I write and read in my room without a lamp, and the huge sleeping buildings in the deserted streets are clearly seen, the Admiralty spire is bright, and dawn hastens to succeed sunset, not letting the night's darkness rise to the golden heavens and leaving a bare half-hour for the night. I love the still air and the frost of your severe winter, the sleighs racing on the banks of the wide Neva...

(From the *Penguin Book of Russian Verse*, 1965, ed. Dimitri Obolensky.)

This plain prose translation gives no idea of the true glory of the Russian poem. (It is to be hoped that Vladimir Nabokov will one day issue a translation of 'The Bronze Horseman' as fine as the verse rendering he has made of 'Eugene Onegin'.) Nevertheless the poem does describe very well the city of Leningrad as it stands today, a second resurrection from nothingness, for Peter's great city had to be almost entirely reconstructed, as was Warsaw after German bombings and extermination campaigns.

While driving down the Nevsky Prospekt we were continually crossing bridges over rivers and canals. Inevitably Leningrad has been called 'The Venice of the north', and indeed there are canals and bridges, quaysides, embarkation steps and various branches of the Neva all over the city. At times, with its groups of eighteenth-century façades set along the calm quays, Leningrad looks like a painting by Canaletto or Guardi, except that there is less animation than in those Italian masters' works, and very little water traffic. However, in the streets of Leningrad I found more vehicular traffic than in any other city of the Soviet Union: there was the ceaseless rumble of trucks and lorries—many carrying what looked like tanks covered rather inadequately by tarpaulins—and there were large numbers of cars, particularly foreign makes bearing tourists from the Baltic countries and Americans from all over the place. Yet this bustle was apparent only in the main streets, Dzerzhinsky Street and Mayorova Prospekt as well as Nevsky Prospekt.

We crossed the Neva by the People's Bridge and passed the Dutch Church, an extremely pretty building modelled on Diocletian's Mausoleum at Split. On the other side of the street was the Stroganov Palace, a lovely eighteenth-century building built by Rastrelli, who was responsible for so much of the best architecture in St Petersburg, as Leningrad was then known.

Another impressive building was also situated on the right of the Nevsky Prospekt, in Kazan Square—the Cathedral of Our Lady of Kazan, set in fine gardens. This was the place where the Red Flag first flew in the centre of the city, on 6th December 1876, at a demonstration by Russian workers under the leadership of the famous political theorist Plekhanov. The colonnade of this now defunct cathedral was copied from St Peter's in Rome, and the main door is a copy of Ghiberti's door of the Duomo in Florence. The interior is filled with glowing gilt icons and trophies of the Napoleonic wars, a noble and touching sight. I was led down into the crypt, which now houses the

Museum of Atheism and which also shows, it is only fair to add, displays of the origins of Christianity, the history of the Papacy and the horrors of the Inquisition. Ancient Greek religion is also fairly well treated here. It is a fascinating museum, and was crowded with a delegation of priests from some Mitteleuropa state when I was there, all of them exclaiming excitedly over the exhibits, which are very well displayed.

After crossing another bridge we stopped farther down the Prospekt at Brodsky Street for a quick look at the souvenir stalls in the Hotel Europe; beyond it lay Arts Square, a lovely complex of buildings by Rossi looking out over gardens and ponds and a fairly recent statue of Pushkin, a great improvement on the one in Moscow. The street is named after the painter Brodsky, who lived at one of the houses which now contains a museum of his works. At the entrance to the square is the Little Opera House, and the northern end is filled by the Russian Museum, commissioned from Carlo Rossi by Alexander I. Later I was to spend almost a whole day in this museum, which, though not as vast and varied as the Hermitage, deserves an extended visit, if only to view the ancient icons so dutifully preserved here, the works of Repin, Serov, Benois and Brodsky and a dazzling display of Revolution propaganda posters. Many of these have recently been published by the Gerhardt Verlag, and they make one ashamed of the weakness of most modern advertising. They have a certain *art-nouveau* charm, and one can see, in their nobly muscled workers and idealized feminine revolutionaries and mothers, the origins of present-day debased Soviet propaganda art.

In the same building is a superb Ethnographical Museum of the Peoples of the U.S.S.R., where I found the display of carpets by the Turkomans of extraordinary refinement both in design and choice of colourings.

There are many fine streets and squares which branch off the Nevsky Prospekt as do Brodsky Street and Arts Square. One of these is Ostrovsky Square with Rossi's Pushkin Theatre and the fascinating Central Theatre Museum devoted to stage plays, opera and Russian ballet. Ostrovsky Square is dominated by an immense monument to the Tsarina Catherine the Great: she looks a proper tyrant, all twelve feet of her, on a massive granite pedestal surrounded by bronze statues of statesmen and generals and one poet, Gavril Derzhavin, who wrote this about his ruler's statue: the poem is called 'The Monument':

I have raised up to myself a wonderful, everlasting monument: it is more solid than metal, higher than the pyramids; neither the whirlwind nor the sudden thunderbolt shall shatter it, nor the flight of time overthrow it...[1]

The poet is also apparently writing about his own Muse, and he refers to Catherine as 'Felitsa' (from the Latin *felicitas*), a sobriquet applied to the empress by her courtiers and admirers. 'The Monument' is a rather fine poem, based on Horace's *Exegi monumentum*, but it has none of the supreme greatness of Shakespeare's sonnet or Pushkin's famous poem on the same theme.

I was impressed by the bronze horses dramatically cabrioling at either end of the next bridge we crossed, the splendid Anichkov Bridge across the Fontanka. Altogether, the Nevsky Prospekt and the streets and squares leading from it are full of great architectural, historical and artistic interest. A drive down the Prospekt from the Admiralty building is one of the best ways to see and understand Leningrad. Combined with the view from the cupola of St Isaac's, it makes one realize that this is essentially a European city, almost without any trace of the Orient or Byzantium. The dignified eighteenth-century buildings of French-Italianate style remind one of Versailles, of Vienna's Schönbrunn and Belvedere Palaces, of Salzburg's Residenz, Heilbroun and Schloss Mirabell, of the parks and palaces of Lazienki and Belvedere in Warsaw, of Berlin's Schloss Charlottenburg and Schloss Bellevue. But even more, Leningrad reminded me of an English city I know well, the city of Bath, which has the same timeless, tranquil air, the lovely rivers, canals and bridges, the superb eighteenth-century architecture and the gentle radiance of Leningrad light. Leningrad is Bath on a grand scale.

So in Leningrad I felt I was already leaving Russia behind, that I was already half way home. It is a city I have come to love with passionate devotion.

---

[1] Gavril Derzhavin: 'The Monument' (from the *Penguin Book of Russian Verse*, 1965, ed. Dimitri Obolensky).

2

THE REAL CAPITAL OF RUSSIA

THE women in Anton Chekhov's *The Three Sisters* looked upon Moscow as an impossible, distant dream city, one they longed for but never really expected to enter out of their provincial dullness. After seeing both Moscow and Leningrad, I wondered why the sister yearned for the former and not the latter. Possibly in 1901, when this play was first produced by the Moscow Arts Theatre, Moscow was a more attractive place than it is now. But it could never have been truly beautiful, as Leningrad undoubtedly still is. I could never yearn to be back in Moscow, but I often dream of returning to Leningrad.

Ever since Peter the Great established this 'window on Europe', as he called it, in 1703, there has been rivalry between Moscow and Leningrad. Today Leningrad is undoubtedly the finer of the two in artistic sensibility, a quality which I found almost totally lacking in hard-headed, practical, rapacious Moscow. There is a grace and gentleness about Leningrad which is due partly, I suppose, to the fact that it *is* a 'window on Europe'. For the first time in Russia I felt that foreign lands were again quite near; in Siberia, central Russia and Moscow I often felt almost suffocated by the sheer vastness of the country I was travelling through: I longed for the smell of other countries and the touch of foreign borders as land-bound mariners long for the sea, as the three sisters longed for Moscow, for some way out of the stifling weight and immensity of Russia. In Leningrad I could breathe again, though still not quite freely.

My guide finished the morning part of the tour by taking me to Revolution Square, where the dignified Basilica of the Holy Trinity is set in pleasant gardens. It was in this basilica that Peter I assumed the title of 'Imperator' in 1711. Along the Petrovsky Quay we came to the modest little house in which Peter the Great lived. It was built in Dutch style in 1703, and was constructed of simple wooden logs. From here Peter supervised the building of St Petersburg. I was touched at the sight of such a small and unpretentious place for so great a man. In his study and dining-room many of the objects he used are still preserved: they too are all simple.

Farther along Petrovsky Quay lay the cruiser *Aurora*, lying at anchor in the Neva. Some Russian sailors were passing by in their white summer uniforms and provided an authentic air. The ship is now a museum. I wanted to visit it, but my guide told me this required a special tour ticket: it could not be included in my general tour of Leningrad. I could have arranged a visit to the *Aurora* through the service bureau at my hotel, but there were so many other interesting, and more lovely, sights that I decided not to waste my time and money on it. Finally, we passed the town house of the Russian ballet dancer Kshessinskaya, a house that was sacked during the Revolution. Near by is a charming mosque, modelled on the Gur-Emir mosque in Samarkand. It was strange to see its two extremely slender minarets rising in those northern skies.

My guide accompanied me to my hotel, where I was to take lunch. I invited him to have lunch with me, but he politely refused. I knew he wanted my Eric Dolphy and Sonny Rollins records much more than any lunch. He had told me that he often taped broadcasts of Western jazz put out by foreign radio stations, though this practice, I found out later, is severely frowned upon by the authorities.

How was I to give him the records inconspicuously? I knew that to invite him to my room would arouse resentment and suspicion on the part of the lady holding the keys. On the other hand, if she saw me go to my room, come out with two long-playing records and then return to my room without them, she would at once guess what had happened. In any case I was already in her black books for trying to take my Japanese girl acquaintance to my room. The only thing to do was to strap the records to my chest: unfortunately there is no sticking-plaster in Russia, as I had found to my cost when I developed a blister on my heel in Moscow and trudged all over GUM Department Store looking for non-existent Band-Aid or its Russian equivalent. All I could do was to fasten the records round my chest with a necktie and hope they did not make me look too square-chested. This I did, and survived the sharp scrutiny of the lady with the keys and the lady working the lift. But as the lift slowly began to descend, stopping for long intervals at every floor, I began to feel the necktie loosening and the records sinking lower and lower. Fortunately I was wearing a rather loosely fitting coat-shirt which concealed fairly well the sharp corners of the record sleeves.

When my guide saw me come out of the elevator into the lobby, he gave me an almost imperceptible sign with his head, meaning 'Follow me'. I followed him to the men's room near the Astoria bar, which, like the bars in all Russian hotels, did not open until nine o'clock in the evening. So the men's room at that hour of noon was quite deserted. I pulled out the records from under my singlet and handed them to my guide, who, smiling for the very first time, stuffed them up his own singlet then buttoned his shirt and jacket tightly across them.

'Thank you,' he said. 'I shall never forget you. I shall never forget your kindness. I have a present for you . . .'

Just as he was reaching into his trouser pocket a hotel porter came in and at once he walked out. After nonchalantly combing my hair, I walked out after him, but when I reached the lobby he was nowhere to be seen. That afternoon, after lunch, he was supposed to come and show me over the Hermitage Museum. He did not turn up. Instead another young man came and took charge of me.

My new guide looked quite modern. He was fashionably dressed, his shoes were clean and not too clumsy, though not as sharply pointed as my own. He was wearing an American nylon shirt and one of those awful American bow ties. He had almost a Beatle haircut, something rather unusual even in more or less libertarian Leningrad. His face was long and pale, with dark brooding eyes and a full but disappointed mouth. Naturally he never smiled. But I liked the look of him: in a nation of well-drilled automata he looked human and refreshingly decadent.

As soon as we met he looked at my shoes. I was not surprised by this, because in Japan I am accustomed to seeing Japanese boys and men look down at my shoes, as if measuring the size, the style and the quality. But this guide's glance meant unmistakably: 'I like your shoes. I want your shoes.' Of course he did not say so.

I do not know how I can possibly do justice to the grandeur and splendour of the Hermitage Museum. My guide raced me through room after room, tapping his feet impatiently whenever I stopped too long in front of a picture or statue. We spent about four hours there that afternoon, and still I did not see everything. I went back alone every day, and spent hours looking carefully at just a few rooms.

The Hermitage Museum was just a short walk from the Astoria Hotel. It stands on one of the finest public square's in Leningrad, the immense Palace Square which witnessed many terrible scenes in the revolutionary history of the city. It was here, in 1879, that Soloviev vainly attempted to assassinate Tsar Alexander II. The infamous massacre of 9th January 1905, when hundreds of workers were shot by troops and police as they approached the Winter Palace to petition the Tsar, took place on Palace Square. It was this tragic event that started the real revolutionary movement in Russia, a movement that was to culminate here also on Palace Square with the storming of the Winter Palace and its occupation by revolutionary troops in October 1917. One side of the square is bounded by a horseshoe-shaped building of great elegance and of enormous size, with a lofty, nobly proportioned Roman triumphal arch at its centre: this is the Red Army Arch, and is adorned by a statue of a conqueror in his chariot. In the clear summer sun this background looked like a stage setting for an Italian comedy of manners. At the centre of the square is Alexander's Column, nearly one hundred and sixty feet high. It is constructed from a single colossal block of granite, and is the biggest monolithic memorial in the modern world. At its summit stands a figure holding a cross. It is in front of this statue that the immense classical frontages of the Winter Palace and the Hermitage extend over an area of more than two thousand five hundred square yards. Beyond them lies the Neva and the quay for steamers departing for Pedrodvorets, the sumptuous summer residence of the tsars, in whose magnificent gardens I was later to spend a dreamy day.

There are said to be over two million art objects in this extraordinary museum called the Hermitage. (What an ironic name this is for such a grandiose and luxuriously decorated building!) At the entrance I bought a catalogue in English entitled *The Treasures of the Hermitage*. This can be obtained in many different languages and costs only one rouble: it is worth the money and is absolutely essential to any serious student of the Hermitage's vast collection.

I was first conducted to rooms displaying the History of Primitive Culture in Russia, and admired chiefly the exquisite Scythian collection of ornaments, jewellery and armour that was discovered in 1830 in Ukrainian tumuli. The display of Russian silverwork was also indescribably lovely, as was the series of Roman portraits and the exhibitions of Hellenic art objects unearthed in the Crimea. There is a large oriental section showing the arts of Tamerlane's Bactrian Period, ancient Egyptian art, a Byzantine collection which is surely the finest in the world, and excellent displays of Chinese, Indian and Japanese classical arts. There were also displays of priceless jewellery, clocks and elaborate trinkets executed by the great jeweller to the tsars, Fabergé. These brought gasps of admiration from the hordes of Russian tourists surrounding me: their reaction to these bourgeois art objects of inestimable worth was envious, not critical.

The rest of the museum, which is divided into two parts, the Little Hermitage and the Old Hermitage (containing Quarenghi's charming little eighteenth-century Hermitage Theatre) is devoted entirely to one of the greatest collections of European art in the world. It includes masterpieces by Leonardo, Raphael, Michelangelo, Titian and my own favourite Italian painter, Giorgione, who is represented by a haunting 'Judith'. The English School holds paintings by Reynolds and Gainsborough and engravings by Hogarth. But the chief glory of this part of the museum is the French collection—entire rooms devoted to the best work of Poussin, Claude, Watteau, Chardin and Hubert Robert, whose paintings of monumental classical ruins must have been much admired in eighteenth-century Leningrad.

Even greater than this wondrous collection of classical French art is the gathering of French Impressionist, Post-Impressionist and later schools: a superb Monet of the Thames, Renoir's delicious 'Lady in Black', Degas's 'Toilette', Cézanne's 'Mont Saint-Victoire', Pissarro, Sisley and hosts of works by Bonnard, Van Gogh, Van Dongen, Marquet, Matisse, Toulouse-Lautrec and Picasso, many of which were represented in the unprecedentedly generous exhibitions of these paintings held in Tokyo in 1966.

It is a good thing to do limbering-up exercises every morning before starting off on one's daily round of the Hermitage's vast galleries, corridors and flights of steps. Even so, one soon sinks into exhaustion and bewilderment and then one can no longer really appreciate the pictures. Then it is good to rest on one of the benches or to go out into the gardens and queue for ice-cream or fruit cordial. I used to sit there on a shady bench, thoughtfully licking a huge cone of ice-cream (the kind which is known in Japan as 'soft ice'), and gaze at the Neva, its banks bordered by one magnificent classical building after another. It is my dream city. If only love too were here it would be perfect. But the people are as of stone. Never a smile, never a spontaneous gesture. And no wonder. This great city was practically razed to the ground during the Second World War by German bombs. Over six hundred thousand people in Leningrad alone died of cold, hunger, bombs, disease. They were interred in two vast communal graves above which burn eternal flames. The rehabilitation of the city in practically its original form is one of the greatest miracles in modern Russia, and the thought of it moved me to tears that salted my soft ice as I gazed upon all the nobility and beauty of the architecture around me.

Across the Neva I could see the infamous bastions of the Trubetskoy Prison, just in front of the Peter and Paul basilica and the Mint in the Peter and Paul fortress. This prison can be visited, for it is now a museum, but I had no wish to go there. Below its grim walls, crowds of people in bathing costumes lay along a narrow beach, basking in the hot sun of the brief Leningrad summer.

I had guessed right. My new guide wanted my shoes. He offered me roubles for them, which I refused, then American dollars, which I also refused. His thin gaunt face seemed to grow even thinner with hidden anguish, cunning and greed. He was like a spoilt child who is denied a sweet or a toy. We were about the same height, and my shoes were the same size as his. Dispiritedly he offered to change my dollars for roubles at four times the official rate, but I was not interested. We were sitting in the Workers' Park near my hotel, smoking rather dry and dusty Russian cheroots. Without saying a word I slipped off my shoes and gave them to him. I did not want his money. I wanted to show him that outside of Russia there are people who will do something for nothing, who despise money and who are not always seeking their own advantage. I walked away in my stockinged feet, leaving him there staring at the shoes and at me. I had left the shoes lying on the ground in front of our seat. As I turned to leave the park I saw him bend down, pick them up and stuff them in his canvas bag.

The pavements of Leningrad were warm under my stockinged feet. People were staring at me as if I were mad. In modern Russia it is considered 'uncultured' and shocking to walk the streets in one's bare feet, because to be without shoes brings one down to the level of the serfs in the 'bad old days' of the Tsarist Empire. But I have been stared at by the ignorant and unimaginative all my life: even the peculiarly stony stares of the Russians did not bother me. I had made a point I had very much wanted to make all the time I was in Russia—that an individual must have freedom of choice and action, and that we must obey unhesitatingly the impulses of our hearts, however unpleasant the consequences. Only thus can we feel free and human instead of like caged beasts.

I got lost the first time I went to the Kirov Theatre. The clerk at the service bureau in the Hotel Astoria had been as good as her word: she had a ticket for *Giselle*. This to me was more precious than gold. She gave me directions about how to reach the Kirov Theatre, which was only about ten minutes' walk from the hotel. I thought I understood her, and to be quite sure I took a map of the city with me, the map provided free by Intourist. But the clerk's descriptions and the map itself were totally inadequate, and clutching my treasured ticket, I soon proceeded to get myself well and truly lost in a maze of small streets, squares, canal banks and bridges behind the Nevsky Prospekt. Of course there were no taxis cruising. It was an unusually warm evening; I began to sweat freely and wished I had ordered a car to take me to the theatre from the hotel. Such cars are very expensive, even for the short distance between the Astoria and the Kirov Theatre, because one had to hire them for the whole evening; they wait outside the theatre for one's return trip to the hotel.

In a square shaded by plane trees I stopped at a small cart on which was a white tank painted with the letters KBAC, pronounced 'kvass'. This, rather than vodka, is the Russian national drink. It is a kind of beer, of very low alcoholic content, brewed from black bread soaked in water, malt, flour and sugar. Russians were standing in line waiting to be served: the drinking of kvass is being encouraged by the Soviet authorities who have grown alarmed at the drunkenness, delinquency and broken homes brought on by the drinking of vodka. The drinking of wine is also being encouraged, with the slogan 'Wine instead of Drunkenness'. This is why vodka is not available on long-distance trains, nor at stations. Louis Pasteur claimed that kvass was invaluable as a medicine, and recently the magazine *Nedelya*, the most popular weekly in the Crimean region, told its readers that the drinking of kvass halts the development of cholesterol in the blood, 'the prime cause of arterial sclerosis and gallstones'. Though it was getting dangerously near the starting time of the ballet performance I was so terribly thirsty after a very salty fish dinner that I joined the queue for a glass of kvass. I was soon served, because both men and women downed their tankards of kvass in one long gulp without stopping for breath. I did so too: it was not unpleasant, but I think I should drink it only if I were desperately thirsty.

I was worried now about reaching the Kirov Theatre on time, because Russian theatres have an admirable rule: at performances of ballet and opera, and at concerts, no one is admitted after the beginning of the performance: one has to wait until the first interval. (This system might well be enforced in Japan, where thoughtless and selfish late arrivals constantly spoil the opening of concerts.)

I was looking about me in perplexity and studying my useless map when someone addressed me in French. It was a charming young lady: I had just been admiring the manly way in which she had swallowed her tankard of kvass, and admiring her luxuriant figure also, which was like the Venus de Milo's. She smiled and said:

'Are you lost?'

'Completely.'

'Where do you wish to go?'

'To the Kirov Theatre.'

At that she flung back her head and gave a full-throated laugh, displaying brilliant, perfect teeth and thrusting out magnificent breasts. I rather feebly joined in her laughter: she was really overwhelming.

Then she took my head between her big, warm hands. For a moment I thought with rapture that she was going to kiss me, but she playfully turned my head until I was looking back over my shoulder.

'There is the Kirov Theatre!' she said, laughing loudly again.

And indeed, the Kirov Theatre was just behind me.

Her fingers were bare of rings, so I judged she was unmarried. Though it is not correct to kiss an unmarried lady's hand, I was so delighted and so grateful that I flung etiquette to the winds, seized her large hand in mine and imprinted a passionate kiss on the back of the wrist. I stammered hastily in French:

'May I see you after the performance? In the bar of the Hotel Astoria?'

She laughed again and nodded, and watched me as I ran for all I was worth towards the big square, Theatre Square, on which the Kirov stands. Before rounding the corner I turned to wave at her, but she had already turned away for another glass of kvass.

It had just gone seven when 1 reached the theatre, and the performance had started. In despair, I showed my ticket to the old lady guarding the door, and, putting my hands together in a gesture of prayer, begged to be let in. She surprisingly relented, and put me in a temporary seat in the back row for the first part of the performance, which was a wonderfully ethereal version of *Chopiniana*, Fokine's first version of *Les Sylphides*. What struck me at once about this particular ballet, so well known as to be totally hackneyed when seen outside Russia, was that the tempo of the music was unusually slow. Even the mazurka and the waltz were taken at slow speeds. This gave a new meaning and intensity to the familiar choreography. The male dancing the Poet was properly languorous in the numbers that called for it, but also displayed great vigour in his leaps: he was a perfect balance of male strength and female sensitivity. Most remarkable of all was the *corps de ballet*, which performed with perfect unison. In particular the beauty and grace of their *port de bras* and the delicacy of their wrists and hands and the relaxed poise of necks and shoulders were revelations of artistry. In all my experience of classical ballet I have never seen anything so exquisitely lovely. The lightness of their feet was also astonishing: every dancer had such a fine *ballon* that even after the highest leap she would come down to the boards softly and lightly as a feather. There was none of the awful thumping one hears in British and American ballet. That lightness was supernatural, almost miraculous in its defiance of the force of gravity. I could well understand now why Nijinsky was famous for his jumps and leaps, for the effect of these movements is greatly enhanced if the dancer returns to the stage lightly, without a sound, and then launches himself with apparent effortlessness into yet another, higher, lingering leap. This is a technique which very few non-Russians have mastered: among men, I can think only of Eglevsky and Nureyev; among women, only Beriosova, and Fonteyn in her earlier years.

Undoubtedly much of the credit for this superb delicacy and lightness is due to the inspired ballet mistress of the company, herself once a famous dancer, Natalia Dudinskaya, a charming woman whom I was to meet later in London at a reception given for the Kirov Company when they danced at Covent Garden. In Covent Garden Opera House I saw the same production of *Giselle* as I saw in Leningrad, with the same magnificent dancers in the leading roles—Natalia Makarova, an enchanting blonde ballerina who seems to be made of spun glass, a fairy drifting on a summer breeze; she was the most perfect Giselle I have ever seen. The Hilarion, Anatole Gridin, was extremely virile, earthy and stocky, and a fine dancer. Albrecht the Prince was the great Soloviev, a dancer of appealing sweetness and gentleness, with a fluidity and grace of movement that reminded me of Nureyev, who also once belonged to this company before his dramatic escape to the West.

I saw other performances: Shostakovitch's *Leningrad Symphony*, choreographed by Belsky, was a bore except for the inspired dancing of Fadicheva and Soloviev. I was familiar with the short act from the ballet *Gayaneh*, for I had seen it danced in Tokyo by Nureyev and Fonteyn, with an unforgettable solo by Fonteyn. Sergei Vikulov was extraordinary for his spins and falls in *La Bayadère*. Irina Kolpakova was enchanting as the Sugar Plum Fairy in *Casse Noisette*.

With all this brilliance of technique and interpretation, it was sad to see such shoddy, ill-constructed, drably painted sets, though they were not quite as bad as the ones I saw at the Bolshoi in Moscow. The costumes too, though not poor, were only just adequate.

I walked back in a dream along the canal banks to my hotel. I half regretted having made a date with the Russian girl, who thought I was French, for I wanted to be alone to savour the enchantment of my memories of the Kirov Ballet. But I had made a promise, and so I must keep it. I hoped she had not got drunk on kvass.

The Astoria Bar is easily the best among the four or five bars that exist in the whole of Soviet Russia. It is dimly lit, and it even has a juke-box. Sometimes young men wearing Castro-type beards or Rolling Stones haircuts would entertain us with songs sung to guitar or balalaika. But I am sure the excellence of the bar depended on the exuberant personalities of the bar-tender and his wife, the vivacious Oleg and his wife Natasha. Oleg is one of the most charming Russians I have ever met; he speaks Russian, Finnish, Estonian, German, French, English and various bits of other languages, including a few phrases of Japanese. He was a good friend to me, making me the most delicious double Screwdrivers with my favourite Stolovaya vodka, and preparing tempting open sandwiches of dark brown bread and smoked salmon, caviar, smoked sturgeon, roast beef or ham. I enjoyed these simple snacks better than anything from the grandiose menus of Russian hotels. I was fascinated by the speed and accuracy with which Oleg changed all kinds of currency and travellers' cheques: he seemed to have an intimate knowledge of every currency in the world. In this bar, as in all the other Russian hotel bars, only 'hard' foreign currency could be used. Oleg was one of the few Russians who would give change in 'hard' currency instead of in roubles and kopeks.

His wife Natasha was a monumental blonde, earthy, maternal, affectionate, happy and extremely muscular—she had once been a champion discus-thrower I was told. There were always a lot of drunks in Oleg's bar, particularly Finnish and Swedish tourists: when one of them became too obstreperous, Oleg would signal to Natasha, who would immediately manhandle him out of the bar. Once when a Russian got drunk, and was found to have no money with which to pay for the drink he had ordered, she seized him by the collar and marched him straight to the police station near the hotel. She had some of the severe charm of Greta Garbo in that enchanting film *Ninotchka*.

Seated on a high stool at the bar, chatting to an amorous young Swede, I found the Russian girl who had spoken to me at the kvass cart. Again she greeted me in French: she had never asked my nationality, and simply assumed from my appearance that I was French. I hadn't the heart to disillusion her: she might not like me at all if I told her I was British. She was drinking Scotch, neat, on the rocks. I asked if I might order her another, and she tossed off the remainder of the whisky in her glass as if it were water.

'Yes, please. A double. Have you a decent cigarette?'

I offered her a 'Peace'. She accepted it wonderingly. I lit it for her she drew on it and puffed out the smoke with a sigh of contentment.

As soon as she had a new drink in front of her we toasted each other, and then she said without warning:

'What I like about you Frenchmen is you are such good lovers. These Americans and Swedes and Chinese don't know how to make love to a girl. They just use her for their own pleasure, never think about *her* pleasure. Americans are just like little boys. They do not give me satisfaction. They're too quick and too rough. I like a bit of sensitivity and self-control in my men. Frenchmen treat a woman like a human being when they make love to her, not like a domestic appliance.'

I sipped my Screwdriver and listened to her extraordinary monologue. She was certainly a passionate, but very sensitive creature.

'I like Japanese men,' she went on. 'They have something no other men have when they're making love. And they've studied all the techniques carefully in ancient books on love-making. The only trouble is', she sighed, 'I keep mistaking Chinese for Japanese. The Chinese are even better than the Japanese at making love, but they are a little too brutal and insensitive. With a Japanese man, even an old man, making love is like painting a picture or writing a poem. I'm crazy about the Japanese business men and tourists who come here. But they seem very timid, as if they're afraid I might gobble them up.'

I was not surprised to hear this, for she was over six feet tall and a really magnificent specimen of Rubens-type beauty. I myself felt I should be utterly lost within her mountainous embrace.

I took her to my room without difficulty. We could stay together no longer than half an hour, because then the chamber-maid would make an excuse to come in and see what we were doing, which was the most delicious love-making I have ever known with a woman. She simply engulfed me in warmth, moisture and perfume, as in a jungle bath. Making love with her was like galloping naked on an unsaddled horse across a gently undulating pastoral countryside full of fresh scents and enchanting sounds. This was the real climax of my stay in Leningrad.

She refused money indignantly, saying she was not a prostitute.

'When I like a man, I take him,' she said. 'That's enough for me. Keep your money, but give me your body, that's my motto.'

Again she broke into that peal of rich laughter that still rings in my ears: she was a true comrade, one I shall never forget, though I never even thought of asking her name, or giving her mine. It would have revealed I was not French. . . .

3
OUT OF RUSSIA

'IF ONLY we could get back to Moscow! Sell the house, finish our life here, and go back to Moscow!'

This quotation from *The Three Sisters* by Chekhov came back to my mind when I was about to leave Leningrad. 'If only we could get back to Leningrad!' was *my* version, for I detested Moscow, and Leningrad was the only Russian city I left with any regret. When the time came for me to leave for Finland, I was most unhappy. But the dates on my visa had to be adhered to strictly, otherwise I should be in trouble.

So early one morning I took a taxi to the Finland station in good time to catch the express that would take me over the frontier into the 'free world', as it is called. Certainly some places are freer than others, or at least one *feels* freer. But for a pacifist-anarchist like myself, there can be no absolute freedom. Everywhere I go I feel caged to some extent, though I always try to do exactly as I please wherever I am.

The express drew into the clean, modern station. It had hardly come to a halt when I heard someone calling my name: 'James! James! James!' Who on earth could it be? I looked round uneasily and could see no one; then I noticed someone beating on the glass of the carriage door and waving and smiling. To my astonishment I saw that it was one of my old friends from Sendai, dear, good Masako Moro! The doors were locked and we were unable to communicate very well, but I gathered she had flown to Moscow from Khabarovsk via Irkutsk, had spent only one night in Moscow, was not stopping at Leningrad, and was now making her way to England, there to stay with some old friends of mine in London. It was an extraordinary encounter, like one of those improbable meetings that are so frequent in Japanese novels by Nagai Kafu or Yasushi Inoue.

Though there was no restaurant car on the train, only a small buffet that was closed all the way, it was quite comfortable, for I had a compartment to myself and I was able to stretch out, strew my things all over the place, drink vodka and nibble the biscuits and the extremely expensive Russian bitter chocolate I had had the foresight to bring with me. As Russian train journeys go, it would not take very long—it was less than a thousand kilometres, and we would be in Helsinki in the late afternoon.

I could have returned to England by the rail-boat route through Hook of Holland (via Brest, one of the oldest towns in Byelorussia, right on the Polish border), but I had booked to come back that way. Or I could have gone to London via Paris on the new international line opened in 1960: this 3,000-kilometre journey takes only fifty hours. But I had decided I wanted to see Scandinavia again, so I was returning by way of Helsinki, Stockholm and Copenhagen.

As I was lolling about reading Proust and sipping Stolnaya a severe-looking gentleman came along the corridor and looked through the window at the book I was reading. He was Russian, probably an agent of some kind. He assumed I was French, and addressed me in that language, which he did not speak very well.

'Why do you read that author?'

'Why shouldn't I?'

'He is a degenerate bourgeois author.'

'He is the finest modern French novelist.'

'His style is unimportant. What he writes is bad. He was a snob. He was also a Jew.'

I was surprised at this.

'What has that got to so with it?' I asked. 'Many Jews are great artists and writers.' I added, maliciously, 'like Chagall.'

'Chagall is decadent,' he said.

'Who are you?' I asked.

He did not reply, so I went on:

'Have you not read Evtuschenko's poem *Babiy Yar*?'

'I know. It is against anti-Semitism. But that poem is not officially approved of, and not admired by our best critics.'

'Nonsense!' I replied. 'I read Evtuschenko's autobiography, and in it he says that the Russian people are not against the Jews.' [1]

'But Proust is anti-Russian, just as Gide became anti-Russian after his visit here.'

---

[1] Evtushenko writes, in *A Precocious Autobiography*: 'Unfortunately it was such people (officials of the Writers' Union) who sometimes made "literary policy", infecting it with evil-smelling things of all sorts, including anti-Semitism. I must say at once that anti-Semitism is not in the least natural to the Russian people, any more than to other people. Anti-Semitism is always grafted on. In

'Proust has very good views on egalitarianism, views that might surprise you. Though he was a Jew, he had Christian charity towards his fellow men, to whatever class they belonged. In some respects Christianity is very close to Marxist ideals, you know.'

I then read him this passage from the second part of *Sodome et Gomorrhe*:

> ... Je n'avais jamais fait de différence entre les ouvriers, les bourgeois et les grands seigneurs, et j'aurais pris indifféremment les uns et les autres pour amis. Avec une certaine préférence pour les ouvriers, et après cela pour les grands seigneurs, non par goût, mais sachant qu'on peut exiger d'eux plus de politesse envers les ouvriers qu'on ne l'obtient de la part des bourgeois, soit que les grands seigneurs ne dédaignent pas les ouvriers comme font les bourgeois, ou bien parce qu'ils sont volontiers polis envers n'importe qui, comme les jolies femmes heureuses de donner un sourire qu'elles savent accueilli avec tant de joie . . .

'Those are not the words of a snob,' I suggested to the gentleman. 'And you should read what Proust says about Tolstoy in this very same book. . . .'

'Show me your passport, please.'

I did not know who he was, but I thought it unwise to provoke him, so I produced my passport.

'You are British!' he said. 'Why did you speak to me in French?' His English was worse than his French.

'It was you who spoke to me in French,' I retorted. 'Just because I was reading a French novel it does not mean that I am French.'

He had no answer to that. He handed back my passport, bowed stiffly and departed.

His dark, severe presence in my compartment had seemed to cloud the sun. When he had gone a certain chill gloom still seemed to linger, and a shiver ran down my spine. What if he had been some kind of literary commissar? The British cultural bureaucrat is horrible enough, as the record of the British Council shows, as the record of the C.I.A.-sponsored Congress for Cultural Freedom shows. But if I had been a Russian thus suddenly detected reading a forbidden work of degenerate French fiction, would I not have been sent to Siberia to work for the

---

Russia it was artificially stirred up under the Tsars, and it was just as artificially stirred up at various times under Stalin. To me, both as a Russian and as a man to whom Lenin's teaching is dearer than anything else in the world, anti-Semitism has always been doubly repulsive.'

(*Penguin Edition*, 1965. Translated by Andrew R. MacAndrew.)

rest of my days in the salt-mines? The thought aroused a nervously perverse giggle in me, and I took another swig of vodka to drive the icy shudders from my marrow. Yet I felt sad and dismayed, and I thought again of all those Russian poets mentioned by Evtushenko who suffered under Stalin. I thought in particular of a strange and erratic woman poet, friend of Pasternak, Marina Tsvetaeva, who went into exile in France, lived there in dire poverty, returned to Russia, could find work only as a charwoman, and in desperation hanged herself. Every government has its own way, obvious or subtle, of suppressing the poets it does not like, as I have found to my cost. It is true what Plato says; poets and governments do not go together: one of them must be exterminated, and it is always the poet. I gave a prayer for the comfort of the soul of Marina Tsvetaeva. About a year later I was to read a very good critical biography of this poor, persecuted creature, *Marina Tsvetaeva: Her Life and Art*, by Simon Karlinsky.[1] She is represented in *The Penguin Book of Russian Verse* by only four brief pieces, all notable for their fierceness and their savage language. What a tiger she must have been! How I wish I had known her! Just look at this description of herself: 'There is an officer's uprightness in my figure, there is an officer's honour in my ribs. I accept any suffering without self-will: there is in me a soldier's patience....'

She sounds very much like myself. Defy the foul fiend of authority! Spit on the bureaucrats of Britain, and of all damned governments in this insane world! Dear Marina Tsvetaeva, I send you my love, and ask you to watch over me... I drink to you!

I have nothing against 'socialist realism' in art, whether in drama, painting or poetry. Art comprehends all things, and it is possible to write great poems on any subject. However, the stress laid by the Russians on 'socialist realism' in art seems to me bad because it reflects something bad—something intolerant and puritanical—that has always existed in the Russian character. I am reminded of Tolstoy's wretched essay on Shakespeare, so brilliantly dissected by George Orwell in 'Lear, Tolstoy and the Fool'.[2] Tolstoy says that a great work of art must be concerned with some theme that is 'important to the life of mankind', and Orwell goes on to resume Tolstoy's ideas thus:

> ... it must express something which the author genuinely feels, and it must use such technical methods as will produce the desired effect. As

---

[1] University of California Press, 1966.
[2] From *Inside the Whale & Other Essays*. Penguin Edition, 1964.

Shakespeare is debased in outlook, slipshod in execution and incapable of being sincere even for a moment, he obviously stands condemned.

This attitude in Tolstoy seems very like the official Soviet stand, its strong disapproval of 'formalism' or art for art's sake. It is not necessary for an artist to be 'sincere' or to discuss themes that are 'important to the life of mankind'. What is important is that he should be able to say what he wants to say in his own peculiar way. Let him be artificial, abstract, didactic, aesthetic, realistic, imaginative, fantastic; only by being himself in his art and in his way of expressing himself in that art will he be sincere. It is not sufficient to 'feel' sincere. The artist must show his sincerity in his performance, not in his emotions or his ideas. No work of art can be entirely perfect, and no artist can be entirely sincere. Sincerity has nothing to do with art, which is largely artifice. What the artist must strive for is a sincere insincerity. But this is something the Soviet cultural authorities, and indeed the cultural despots in most countries, will not admit.

I love the satirical tales of Mikhail Zoschenko, and his remarkable autobiography, *Before Sunrise*. He was a writer who was constantly persecuted by authorities and cultural dictators. He is very like Pasternak when he writes, towards the beginning of his autobiography, these revealing words: 'The world is horrible, I thought. People are cheap and vulgar. Their behaviour is comical. I don't run with the herd...'

'I don't run with the herd.' That is like Pasternak's reference to himself as a 'white cormorant'. In Soviet Russia, and in all lands, those who do not run with the herd are condemned from the start: but more so in Russia than anywhere else excepting, perhaps, Japan. Perhaps this is the reason for the profound melancholy I have noticed in so many Russians and Japanese: this melancholy is rather a profound sense of resignation, a passive acceptance of the inevitable. In this respect, Russians are very oriental.

Zoschenko quotes Kant and Aristotle: 'My favourite philosophers referred to melancholy respectfully. "Melancholics possess a sense of the exalted," wrote Kant. And Aristotle believed that "A melancholy turn of mind aids profound thought and accompanies genius".' [1]

He gives many quotations from great Russian melancholics: Gogol, Nekrasov, Andreyev, Saltykov-Shchedrin, Briusov and L. N. Tolstoy, who wrote, in *The Truth about my Father*: 'It seems to me that my life has been a stupid farce.' Many of them talk bitterly about an unfulfilled

[1] *Nervous People and Other Stories* by Mikhail Zoschenko, ed. Hugh McLean. New York. Vintage Russian Library, 1965.

longing to commit suicide. No wonder this brilliant autobiography, so very unsocialist and unrealistic, was suppressed by the Soviet literary censors!

Yet all these writers whose freedom was somehow or other destroyed or limited remain paradoxically free. Even Marina Tsvetaeva, according to an account by Nina Berberova in *The New York Review of Books*, is beginning to be read again in the Soviet Union, and her works are gradually creeping back into print. True genius can never be suppressed by any state, true individuality finally comes to be seen as essential to even the most authoritarian government. But the terrible crushing force of Stalinism remains. In Milovan Djilas's [1] interesting *Conversations with Stalin* there comes this very important passage:

> In his own country Stalin had subjected all activities to his views and to his personality, so he could not behave differently outside. Having identified domestic progress and freedom with the interests and privileges of a political party, he could not act in foreign affairs other than as a dictator. And like everyone else he must be judged by his actual deeds. He became himself the slave of the despotism, the bureaucracy, the narrowness, and the servility that he imposed on his country.

It is indeed true that no one can destroy another's freedom without losing his own.

I am again reminded of an autobiography, one of the greatest ever written, by Maxim Gorky. In his *Childhood* he writes (I quote from the French translation of Davydoff and Pauliat): [2]

> C'est ainsi que prit fin mon amitié avec Bonne-Affaire. Il fut le premier que je rencontrai parmi ces hommes innombrables qui se sentent étrangers dans leur propre pays et sont pourtant les meilleurs d'entre nous . . .

And:

> Plus tard, j'ai compris que les Russes, dont la vie est morne et misérable, trouvent dans leurs chagrins une distraction. Comme des enfants, ils jouent avec leurs malheurs dont ils n'éprouvent aucune honte.
>
> Dans la monotonie de la vie quotidienne, le malheur lui-même est une fête et l'incendie un divertissement. Sur un visage insignifiant, même une égratignure semble un ornement.

These quotations from Gorky seem to me to sum up all my feelings about the Russians of today.

*   *   *   *   *

[1] *Conversations with Stalin*. Penguin Books, 1963.
[2] *Enfance*. Livre de Poche. Paris, 1959.

I turned from my melancholy thoughts, washed my face, brushed my hair and felt much better. I had my own little private bathroom and toilet in which I could have taken a shower had I so wished, but the water was cold. I contented myself with a few more slugs of vodka as I lounged about, scribbling poems and gazing out of the windows. The landscape was flat and green, pastoral, a-shimmer with silver birches, gloomed with pines. The immense, pale sky was awash with light, as if stained by a white radiance thrown back from innumerable lakes or from a foam-flecked ocean. There were frequent stretches of lake water among the silver birches, and still I could sense in the distance, like the far-away beating of a muted drum, the white expanse of Lake Ladoga. This particular stretch of landscape has been perfectly evoked, in all its mysterious winter silence, by Curzio Malaparte in *Kaputt*, his great novel about the struggles between Finns and Russians during the Second World War . . . the wind of the north in Karelia . . . ice on the River Kodima . . . the horses frozen into Lake Ladoga . . . the snowy town of Viipuri, capital of Karelia, once Finnish, now Russian, and renamed by the Russians with its Swedish name of Vyborg.

This is the frontier town between Russia and Finland. We were approaching it around noon. There was a long stop, during which we could get off the train and change our remaining roubles into Finnish money; this was our last chance to buy Russian souvenirs, but by now I was sick of the sight of amber, *matryushka* dolls and fur caps. Only vodka still held my affections, and I bought a new bottle.

Vyborg from the railway looked snug and peaceful in the summer sun—a far cry from those terrible winter nights of war described so feelingly by Malaparte.

Then the train crossed the frontier. The landscape was just the same, but I felt a distinct lightening of tension. I took a deep breath. Finnish immigration officers came and examined my passport. They were pleasant young men with fresh, ruddy, open faces and quiet smiles. After glancing at my passport and stamping it, they handed it back and gave me a graceful salute. Yes, this was the feeling of the 'free world'—the sense of an oppression lifted. The doors between the carriages were unlocked, and I was able to go and chat with Masako Moro. By another strange coincidence we were booked into the same hotel, the Hospiz in Helsinki.

I spent three days in Helsinki. What a relief it was to be there after Russia! The shops were full of every kind of good thing. No one was queuing, no one was pushing and shoving to buy a few bruised tomatoes or apples. The market square down by the harbour near the quayside where the steamers depart for Turku and Stockholm was crammed with stalls arranged picturesquely round the fountain of Havis Amanda, the mermaid representing Helsinki rising from the waves, like a northern Aphrodite. These stalls were loaded with the most perfect fruit, berries, vegetables and flowers: a sight unthinkable in Russia. The fish market was awash with an infinite and plenteous variety of fish.

After enjoying a sauna bath, at the end of which I was deliciously flogged with birch twigs by an old woman like my great-grandmother, I went to the roof restaurant of a large hotel near the Station Square and, after a few glasses of schnaps, ordered the specialty of the season—lovely fresh-water crayfish washed down with more schnaps and beer. The waiter serves me at once, is attentive and friendly. He says, charmingly, in English:

'Do you want much more?'

This was after I had devoured a dish of a dozen succulent crayfish and downed six glasses of schnaps and beer.

He was most concerned because I did not want any more.

'Are you ready now?' he asked, meaning: 'Have you finished now?' It is curious that I heard this English phrase, 'Are you ready now?' used by both Russians and Finns after the completion of the sexual act.

There is a great thoroughness and conscientiousness in the Finnish character. For example, in order to avoid staining my shirt and jacket, while eating the splashy crayfish, I was presented with a frilly plastic apron, which the kind waiter tied on for me, and a pair of frilly plastic cuffs, whose terribly tight elastic sent my blood-pressure soaring. This is the essence of the Finnish character—solid and dependable and unyieldingly courageous, an essence which is expressed in their word *sisu*.

I was glad to be out of Russia. But was Finland, after all, so very different from the Soviet Union? Of course I was happy to be in Helsinki, and felt I was lucky to be able to travel freely, something most Russians cannot do. I spent a perfect day visiting a model suburb called Tuonela, self-centred and very modern, all fountains and gardens and fine roads and immense blocks of flats. It seemed very nice and all that, but to live there every day must be like existing in a functionalized, life-supporting desert. I think of those huge apartment complexes, almost exactly the same as the moon landscapes of outer Moscow and Leningrad, as 'breeding-blocks'.

The farther one travels west, the more deserted cities appear to be. As one comes to richer nations, like the Finnish, the quieter the town centres, the feebler the social life of the streets and squares. I think that all this modern urban planning, so well-intended, has not only distributed more evenly centres of dense population, it has also diluted something human and essential, the sense of community; it has disintegrated the soul as well as the social warmth and energy of man. We are all in the West gradually being enfeebled by isolation and regimentation. I think of the prophetic nature of Louis MacNeice's splendid poem, 'Prayer Before Birth':

> ... I fear that the human race may with tall walls wall me,
>   with strong drugs dope me, with wise lies lure me,
>   on black racks rack me, in blood-baths roll me ...
>
> ... I am not yet born; O fill me
>   With strength against those who would freeze my
>   humanity, would dragoon me into a lethal automaton,
>   would make me a cog in the machine, a thing with
>   one face, a thing, and against all those
>   who would dissipate my entirety, would
>   blow me like thistledown hither and
>   thither or hither and thither
>   like water held in the
>   hands would spill me
> Let them not make me a stone and let them not spill me.
> Otherwise kill me.

This, the only really great poem MacNeice ever wrote, could well be applied to life in Japan, in China, in Russia, in Finland, in Sweden, in Denmark, in Britian, in the United States.... How can we stop this 'dissipation'? Only by resolving to remain individuals in spite of everything.

In the Helsinki Parliament House five gilded near-nude statues are grouped together in the main assembly hall: only one of them is female, and, holding a child in her arms, is said to represent the future. But—she stands with her arse to the assembled members.

Out in the sunny streets everyone looks alike, except for a sudden radiant vision of countrywomen—are they in native dress, or are they gypsies?—wearing beautiful full, lacy skirts, ankle-length—blue, red, yellow—with frilly blouses, long hair. These peasant women give off an air of sweetness and wholesomeness. But they smirk modestly as I catch their eye, and swing their hips as they saunter past me, suggesting also the calm, resourceful life of village gossips.

I become aware at once of the translucent, transparent, pure, elusive, clean and clinical quality of Helsinki. I begin to hate the almost paralysing perfection of modern buildings, equipment, accommodation, accessories, services. At night it is a city of lighted glass blocks and boxes. After 8 p.m. on weekdays, and all day on Sundays, the streets are virtually empty. Such abstraction numbs the heart, such empty perfection chills the soul.

I am not surprised at the beat protest in modern life, though here in Helsinki it seems to be just a gesture, quiet, tame, conventional. The Finnish beats are all conformists. They hang around the Student House and along the tree-lined Boulevard leading down to the quayside. They have shoulder-length hair and go barefoot in summer (as do many children in Tuonela, the garden suburb). There is a dullness in the air. Not for nothing do the Finns call their land Suomi, which means 'swamp'. The collection of hippies round the cinema in Mannerheim Mintie and round the statues of Mannerheim and Einoleino hardly seem to be really alive, as if they were slowly being suffocated by the rarefied perfection of dullness that is their city. I missed the dirt and noise and packed pavements of Tokyo very much.

Yet I was glad to see signs of rebellion among the young, signs that would not be allowed at all in Soviet Russia. Young men with long blond hair flowing right down to their shoulder-blades were a very common sight. They wore old, dirty clothes and wandered around the street with filthy bare feet. Young women too went barefoot, and their beautiful moonlight-coloured hair was dulled by dirt, bedraggled, matted.

It was in Helsinki too that I saw my first mini-skirts, with hems about four inches above the knees. The Finnish girls have long, slender, pretty legs, and look enchanting in this type of dress.

I took some trips out into the countryside round Helsinki, and to some of the many islands and bays, where one can eat good food in excellent but expensive restaurants like the Kalastajatorppa, the Casino on the island of Kulosaaren and the Walhalla on the island of Sveaborg. Out in the country away from the city I could feel some of the true spirit of Finland, as it is expressed in the works of the great composer Sibelius. In the woods and forests, walking by lonely bays and streams, it was easy to imagine the legendary heroes of Finland like Lemmenkainen—noble, brave and austere—and the Swan of Tuonela.

I went by boat to Stockholm. There was an excellent dining-room on board, and one could buy all kinds of wines and spirits free of tax. I bought a bottle of Scotch and a large bottle of Russian vodka. The crossing at night was extremely comfortable.

I had not bothered to reserve a room at any hotel in Stockholm because I knew from experience that a hotel room would be easy to find. One has only to go to the hotel reservation booth on the quayside or to the one in the Central station and one is immediately told where there are hotels with vacant rooms. I often wish that this sort of service could be obtained in Japanese cities. I asked for a room at one of my favourite hotels—the modest, homely, quiet Eden Hotel in Sturegatan, overlooking the Humle Garden. There was a long, geranium-decked balcony outside my window; it ran the whole length of the building, connecting all the rooms. I left my bottle of vodka on my dressing-table beside the open window and went out for a walk. When I got back the bottle had been stolen. Someone had obviously walked along the balcony, seen the bottle, reached through the open window and lifted it. I was curiously shocked by this. I know the Swedes are terrible drunkards, but I did not think they stole in order to get liquor; the person who took it must have been desperate for a drink. I hope it gave him a monumental hangover. This was something that would never have happened in Russia or Japan.

When I reported the theft at the reception desk downstairs the clerk made no effort to do anything. He plainly disbelieved my story. I complained to a policeman who was passing outside, but he only laughed, and—gave the Russian shrug. This restored my sense of perspective. I laughed too and gave my own peculiar, hopeless, helpless form of the shrug.

I found that the cafés and gardens at the centre of the city were almost entirely occupied by throngs of long-haired boys and short-skirted girls who never seemed to do any work. They just lounged about in the sun, combing their hair and their beards and chatting resignedly about the Red Guards in China, the war in Vietnam, the dreadful famine in India and the Negro riots in the U.S.A. There were many Negroes and Arabs and Middle Eastern youths in the cafés of the Vasapark, ogling the fresh-complexioned and wildly pretty Swedish girls with their heavenly pale blonde hair. For the most part these young people seemed completely apathetic towards the problems they were discussing. Like Japanese students, they felt that it was enough to discuss such things, to show one was 'with it'. The most they ever did was to sign petitions. They were demonstrating the fact that in this world one can do nothing, and that the Buddhist philosophy of non-action is the root of all good. I saw my American hippie, by an extraordinary coincidence, lounging with a large group of Swedish hippie friends at the tables of an outdoor café. He saw me too I was sure, though we were at least a hundred yards apart. But we exchanged no sign of recognition. In the lives of hippies and wanderers like myself, personal encounters are without much importance.

England was getting nearer, and I was getting unhappier. I crossed from Sweden to Denmark by ferry, and landed in Denmark at Helsingor, whose great castle on the sea is the Elsinore of Shakespeare's *Hamlet*. The town was packed with tourists eating substantial Danish meals and quaffing pint after pint of Danish lager. The castle too was crowded: there was no likelihood of the ghost appearing in its magnificently restored banqueting hall, at least not during the summer tourist season. But I could well imagine ghosts appearing there in the misty, icy Danish winter and haunting those sombre walls and staircases.

In Copenhagen I was horrified to find, a few steps from those delightful pleasure gardens known as Tivoli, a frightful imitation British pub. England was certainly getting closer, too close for pleasure. The imitation British pub was awfully good as an imitation— stale cheese sandwiches, lukewarm beer and darts in a subdued atmosphere of jovial melancholia. I prefer the 'Guinness Pubs' in Tokyo's Ginza and Shinjuku.

But the most extraordinary sight in Copenhagen was the large number of young tramps and hippies and bogus 'artists' from various countries. (I noticed there were none from Communist territories.) These creatures were earning a precarious living by drawing pictures and writing poems on the roads. Near the City Square there are two fairly narrow streets that have been closed to traffic. They are called Frederiksberggade and Gammeltorv, and all along these two streets are young men and women, mostly barefoot, with long filthy hair and wearing extremely dirty clothes, who sit for hours beside the usually very poor pictures they have drawn in coloured chalks on the road.

These people have become one of Copenhagen's main tourist attractions. Their pictures are always accompanied by naïve messages such as: 'I am a poor art student from France. I want to travel to Kyoto in Japan to become a Zen Buddhist monk. But I have no money and I can't find work in Copenhagen. Please help me by giving me lots of money and you will receive the blessings of Buddha. Thank you.' Beside this message would stand a begging-bowl or a hat into which passers-by, mostly tourists, would throw a few coins.

The dishonesty, insincerity and cynicism of these bogus students were obvious: yet the tolerant Danish Government allowed them to stay there defiling the streets with their tasteless pictures. Tourists, amused and taken aback by such egotism and effrontery, encouraged the fakes to perpetuate their sham by throwing them money and cigarettes.

I was sorry to see two groups of Japanese young men begging in this discreditable way. One group was dressed in university or high school uniforms: they had drawn small coloured squares on the road marked: 'Put money here. Put cigarettes here. Put matches here.' Needless to say they couldn't speak a word of English or any other language but Japanese.

The other Japanese group presented an even more absurd appearance, for they were dressed in *yukata* or cotton summer kimono, or in judo costume, and wore *geta*. Two of them had a pair of *geta* made apparently of cast-iron, which they were using as dumb-bells. From time to time they would give a very feeble judo demonstration. Before them on the road was the picture they had drawn in coloured chalks—a crude and inaccurate copy of a famous painting by Utamaro, enlarged to the fantastic dimensions of ten feet by six. When I tried to take a photograph of it, one of the Japanese stopped me, saying: 'Give me five dollars.' This was the fee they charged for permission to photograph the picture. They would not allow me to snap their faces. When I told them that I lived in Japan and gave them my name-card, they refused to tell me their names.

I had the feeling that they and the other young people were not true artists, for a true artist cannot afford to waste his time and energy in such a pointless way. Rather I felt that they were just obeying a fashion or conforming to a type of behaviour which young people today think is clever and picturesque. It is all a pose, and not a pretty one. I was to see examples of such behaviour all over England. It would certainly not be allowed in Russia, or seen in Japan, whose hippies are dying out.

I journeyed by train ferry from Copenhagen to Hook of Holland. The food on that continental express was quite abominable, as was the real British grub served on the night ferry from Hook of Holland to the port of Harwich, where I finally set foot again on my native soil. I felt no emotions beyond a faint nausea on returning to the land of my fathers. (I can still remember Dylan Thomas, drunk as a lord, yelling scornfully in the streets of Soho: 'Land of my fathers! They can bloody well keep it!')

I was wearing my C.N.D. badge when I passed through Immigration. After my passport had been checked, and I was leaving the Immigration counter, a high official and a plain-clothes detective came running after me and demanded to see my passport again. The official checked my name in a mysterious black book containing thousands of names, and then I heard him whisper disappointedly to the plain-clothes man: 'No, that's not him.' Chiding him gently for using such bad English grammar I drifted to the cafeteria for a cup of tea and found that the price of 'cups that cheer but not inebriate' had doubled since my last visit to England in 1964. I now had to pay almost as much as I would pay for a cup of coffee in a Japanese coffee-shop. No wonder England was having a severe financial crisis!

I bought *The Times*, the *Guardian* and the *Daily Telegraph* to read on the train. Their price had also gone up. The newspapers informed me that Harold Wilson's inept Labour Government would have to devalue the pound. Britain was in the throes of financial catastrophe, and wholesale sacking, short time and protest strikes were already grim realities.

I threw aside the papers in disgust and boredom, and gazed out at the Essex countryside through which we were speeding. It was looking very lovely and very British: the moderate sun was shining on trim, calm green meadows bordered with low hedges and leafy elms and poplars. We roared through sedate little country towns like Colchester and Chelmsford, then finally began to enter the dull, smug suburbs of smoky London. As we reached the centre of the city, and the train began to approach Liverpool Street station, I noticed many ugly new buildings and factories among the wretched, dingy workers' hovels.

Despite the financial crisis there is in England, as in Japan, a building boom and a mania for reconstruction. I was saddened to learn that one of my picturesque old haunts, Piccadilly Circus, is soon to be torn down and reconstructed as a vast plaza in some anonymous continental style of architecture. I recalled the severely modern characterless squares and city centres of Helsinki and Stockholm, and regretted that the lively, gay, Bohemian centre of the West End of London was to be desecrated in this way, turning it into one of those grim townscapes of George Orwell's novel *1984*, a date which is now not so very far away.

PART FIVE

BACK TO TOKYO

I

THE JOURNEY BACK

I RETURNED to Moscow by way of Hook of Holland, Berlin, Warsaw, Brest, Minsk and Smolensk. I travelled in a state of hyper-anxiety because of my lack of a re-entry permit for Japan. I went to the Japanese Embassy in Grosvenor Street hoping to straighten things out there before I was due to leave. They were extremely kind to me. They telephoned and cabled to Tokyo in an attempt to get my permit in time, but day after day went by and still it did not arrive. The embassy knows me well, and I showed them my contract with Japan Women's University and the official card that states I am a professor of that university. But all to no purpose. The law must be obeyed to the letter. The embassy officials advised me to delay my return to Japan for a week or so.

This of course was impossible. In the first place, when travelling through Russia one has to stick exactly to the schedule that is made out for one on visas and tickets. One must catch a certain train or plane and no other. If one fails to observe the regulations of the time-table, one is in trouble. I had no wish to get into hot water with the Russian officials and Intourist.

Secondly, I had to be back in Tokyo in time to mark my students' examination papers and to begin my new classes. It was unthinkable that I should let my devoted and darling Japanese students down: I might let down a student of some other nationality with a light heart, but never a Japanese.

In Japan there is always some way to get round a law. Japanese laws seem made to be circumvented. I carefully sounded the Japanese Embassy officials on the possibility of getting to Japan on time. I could enter Japan at any time as a tourist, they told me, without any special visa. But I could stay only six weeks. If I wanted to stay longer I should have to go to Hong Kong and get my entry permit from the Japanese Embassy there. This I was quite prepared to do. Hong Kong is only three hours' flight from Tokyo, and I always like spending a week-end there. So I left for Russia on time and without difficulty.

The journey was uneventful. I had a carriage to myself all the way from Hook of Holland to Berlin and Warsaw. As the train approached Warsaw towards the end of that October afternoon I was filled with foreboding. Would I like it? The sight of a Stalin-type wedding-cake structure in the distance did not encourage me.

I stayed at the Europejski Hotel, a fairly new hotel. It was quite pleasant, with an indifferent restaurant and a poor bar. I used to go out for meals to the café-restaurant on the eleventh floor of the Grand Hotel, which is easily the best in Poland, and gives a wonderful night view of the city. The bar at the Orbis-Bristol Hotel was not bad: I found out that the Poles serve bottled beer at three temperatures: lukewarm, cold and heavily chilled—the latter reserved for Americans.

From the window of my hotel I could see the park—at night surely the darkest in Europe and the least unfrequented—with an eternal flame burning under an arch guarded by two motionless armed soldiers. I visited the wonderfully reconstructed old town, whose beautiful cobblestoned Market Square was wiped out by the Nazis. There is a fine restored cathedral, the Pod Blacha Palace and the charming, rebuilt red-brick Barbican with towers and walls, all very medieval.

In this ancient market-place with its fine gables and pretty wrought-iron shop signs there is a famous restaurant, the Krokodyl, and a wine-shop, Fukier's, both of which I visited and enjoyed.

I was amused by the young couples in Warsaw coffee-shops and bars and restaurants. For them a rendezvous was obviously something special: they would sit opposite each other, their heads close together, staring earnestly into each other's faces, talking with great seriousness. The girl would have a whole repertoire of facial expressions—pouts, sad smiles, raised eyebrows, amused frowns, eyes suddenly shut or opened wide—as if she felt she were the star in some new Polish movie. She would run the whole gamut of these expressions, with her male making a number of supporting gestures and faces, rather like a male dancer doing a *pas de deux* with an over-emotional ballerina. They would both obviously be enjoying themselves tremendously, even when the lady shed a few tragic tears. I have never seen people talk to each other with such idiotic intensity, as if they alone existed in the world. It was all highly self-conscious, yet it was not done for the benefit of others, only for themselves.

I disliked Warsaw. I thought it was drab and dull. It was worse than Moscow. At least in Russia I had made a few friends with Russians and Africans and Japanese, but here there was no one. There was a sense of utter blankness. I did not care for the Polish art on display in museums and galleries, though I saw an exhibition of posters which I thought were perfect. The churches lacked mystery and, like the people, were chilly. There is no 'Warsaw shrug'. It is not necessary. The Varsovians are simply indifferent to others, locked away permanently in themselves. The only time anyone spoke to me was when they thought I might have some dollars to exchange for zlotys.

The parks are lovely, and I admired the palaces of Lazienki and Belvedere, but somehow it all seemed to be behind impenetrable layers of plate glass. I made a rapid bus excursion round the city with an excitable, ravaged, passionate Polish woman as our guide. Her skull-like smile still haunts me, and her blazing eyes and guttural Polish accent. While we were driving from one sight to another she would regale us with tales of the atrocities committed by the Germans. From time to time she would smile her death's-head smile and say:

'I do hope there are no Germans on this tour. Of course I know there are good people in all nations, just as there are bad people. So if there are any good Germans with us today I hope they will forgive me, but naturally I must tell the truth about what they did to us Poles during the Nazi Occupation. This is something that we Poles shall never forget, and never forgive!'

Her deep-sunken eyes in their dark pits of flesh blazed with pale blue ferocity, like splinters of electrified ice. Fortunately there were no Germans with us that day. She went on:

'Even when there *are* Germans with us I speak the truth! I must speak out! I must tell you what they did to us!'

She was a terrifying but impressive lady. I could not help admiring her. She often referred to the Germans as 'Krauts', and not in the half-humorous, half-affectionate way this term is applied to people like Marlene Dietrich and Erich von Stroheim. She spat it out with diabolical hatred.

She took us to a house in the old Market Square where we were shown a perfectly revolting film of German atrocities in Warsaw, a film that brought tears of pity and fury to my eyes. I could not believe that such human suffering was possible. The fate of the gentle, dark-eyed Jews in the Warsaw ghetto was indescribably hideous.

'Now if there are any Krauts in our audience', the Polish lady's ringing voice came from the back of the auditorium, 'you will see them rushing for the exit.' Several people were indeed running for the doors, but they were not Germans. They were wanting to be violently sick. The Warsaw authorities have thoughtfully provided basins outside the doors for such emergencies. It was all unspeakably painful, and I began to realize why the Poles were so dour and icy: they had been several times through hell, and war had steeled their hearts against everything. They had become so hard that now nothing could hurt them again. And in those hearts hatred and revenge smouldered magnificently, as they did in the heart of that Polish guide. I could easily imagine her as a heroine of the Polish resistance, indomitable, daring, mad with suppressed rage and venom and desire to kill every German she could lay hands on. Her references to the Russians were hardly less outrageous: she could never forgive them, she said quite openly, for not coming to the assistance of the Polish Resistance when the Germans were being driven out at last.

The awfulness of that war still seemed to hang over Warsaw. It hung over the ludicrous Palace of Culture and Science too—the wedding-cake architecture that was a gift from Stalin to the heroic citizens of Warsaw. Those citizens have a sharp sense of the ridiculous, and they say that the best view of Warsaw is from the top of this monstrous edifice, because then you cannot see it. It contains innumerable cinemas, restaurants, dance halls and an extremely tedious night-club in the basement. The war still seemed to hang over the sad River Vistula, along whose deserted banks I often strolled when the oppressive sadness of the city grew too much for me. The gloom extended to the new housing projects of Marszalowska, another example of human disintegration, like an immense cemetery for the living who are provided with kindergartens, schools, hospitals, club rooms and cultural centres—what could be more killing to culture than a 'cultural centre'? There were no churches.

Food seemed a little better than in Russia. There seemed to be more things obtainable in the shops, but even so the range was limited. A number of shops in the main streets, Krakowskie Przedmiescie and

Nowy Swiat, contained foreign articles, either new or second-hand, which could be bought at a high price. Near the Palace of Culture and Science there was a row of small shops selling cheaper goods—drab clothes, caps, boots, tools and all the impedimenta needed in do-it-yourself drudgery—for the Poles are wonderful at knocking things up out of nothing. They are great home-makers. The men are thoroughly domesticated, pushing prams, carrying shopping-bags, hunting for bargains during lunch time, queueing for a few rare plums or lemons or bruised bananas. A sense of squalor and desolation is ever present. I remember the gaiety of the members of the Polish Ballet who came to perform in England during the Second World War: where has all that zest and gaiety gone? Perhaps it can be found at village feasts and weddings. Certainly it is missing in the capital and in Krakow, a city that is little more than a living museum. The lilt and the elastic *rubato* have gone out of the mazurka, the nobility and vigour have died in the polonaise. Chopin was born outside Warsaw, at Zelazowa Wola. His ghost haunts this desperate, sad city.

The journey from Warsaw to Moscow was also uneventful. We had a long stop at Brest, the frontier town, where a Japanese pianist I had met on the train kept me company. I was surprised to see that two officials took him aside and asked for his passport in a very unfriendly manner. However, he kept calm and the incident passed over. We went to the buffet for some very dull rolls and cheese and beer. I got a bottle of very fine Polish vodka, Polmos Zubrowka, Bison Brand Vodka 'flavoured with an extract of Zubrowka, the fragrant herb beloved by the European bison, 40° proof'. This is a state monopoly. It says on the screw-cap: *Panstwowy Monopol Spirytusowy*. It is excellent drunk neat, each mouthful followed by a sip of ice water. Recently I have found bottles of this splendid spirit in the wine department of Isetan Department Store in Tokyo. I am extremely fond of it. It is, for me, the best thing to come out of Poland.

This time I was staying at the immense Ukraina Hotel in Moscow. It is a daunting place. Here too it is hard to get served in the restaurants. One evening, after waiting one hour for the waitress to bring my bill, I simply got up and walked out. No one bothered about me. I had that meal free of charge.

Two incidents remain firmly in my memory. After having been constipated for a few days I suddenly had a call of nature. I did not want to wait until I got to my room—it took easily ten minutes to reach my floor by lift—so I dashed into a public toilet on the second floor. An old dame was in charge, fussing about wiping things and handing out fistfuls of toilet-paper with a disgruntled look. I delivered myself of a particularly rich and massive turd. When I tried to pull the flush I found it would not work. I tugged and tugged, and finally a miserable trickle of water came, not sufficient to flush away my prize exhibit. I could do nothing about it, so I just left it. The old dame was hovering ominously beside the door as I came out, with a rag in her hand, ready to rush in and wipe the seat. When she saw the Christmas box I had left behind me she gave a howl of indignation and treated me to a stream of Russian curses which stopped the other Russians in the wash-room dead in their tracks. They gazed at me in open-mouthed horror, as if I had desecrated Lenin's Tomb. I heard them muttering the Russian word for 'uncultivated' or 'uncultured person', which is one of the deadliest insults one can offer anyone in Russia.

What did I do? I gave the Russian shrug, and made my exit with a dazzling smile, waving a fond, regretful farewell to the old dame, who had dashed out to fill a bucket with water which she now proceeded to fling into the toilet-bowl as if she were dousing a conflagration of the first magnitude. Everything happens to me!

The second remarkable event of my second visit to Moscow was my sighting of an unidentified flying object for the first time in Russian skies. I had previously sighted U.F.O.s three times in Japan—once in Sendai in 1960, once on a ferry making the night crossing between Aomori and Hakodate also in 1960, and once in Japan's southernmost island of Kyushu, where I saw three objects flying in a row, in a half-clouded sky, from Shimabara.

I never expected to see an unidentified flying object in Russia. But see it I did, from my window on the twenty-sixth floor of the Hotel Ukraina, on the night of 20th–21st September. I had gone to bed about midnight after the usual mysterious telephone call from a jabbering Chinese call-girl. Soon I fell asleep, but at about 2 a.m. I was wakened from sleep by the occupant of the next room taking a prolonged and very noisy bath. (As in most Japanese hotels, the walls of Russian hotels are rarely completely soundproof.) I am a very light sleeper, and as the man next door seemed to be drunk and was taking a long time over his ablutions, I got out of bed and went to the window, whose curtains were drawn.

I had often admired the view of the sinuous Moskva River from my window in day time. This was the first time I had looked out on Moscow at night from my room. It was a magnificent sight. There was very little traffic in the streets, which lay brilliantly lighted among the big blocks of apartments. It was a night of low cloud. Towards the horizon, on my left, I saw the huge bulk of Moscow University with the five big red stars at the top of its pinnacles. I was gazing at these red stars when, to my surprise, the one on the extreme left began to move; or at least I thought at first that it was the star moving. But then I realized that it was a light moving behind the red star-topped towers. It was exactly the same red colour as the stars adorning the pinnacles and was flying very fast, very low on the horizon, in a westerly direction from Moscow University. As it flew the red light changed to white then back to red, then to white, alternately, in a regular pulsing rhythm. While the white light shone it seemed to hover; when the red light shone it shot forward. The object disappeared behind a large block of apartments on the horizon. I knew it could not be a plane showing its landing lights, for there is no airfield in that direction, and when the object passed behind the apartment block I could see the white light casting an intermittent glow on the low-lying clouds above the dwellings.

Next morning there were no reports of any such objects in the newspapers. But I sent a number of postcards to various friends in Europe and Japan telling them quite openly the details of what I had seen. All these cards reached their destination, and were not censored in any way.

In Leningrad I had seen a well-sung but boring production of *The Magic Flute* at the pretty Kirov Theatre. In Moscow this time I was lucky to get a seat for *Sorochinski Fair*, which I remembered having seen once before in England during the war with a remarkable Russian singer, Olga Slobodskaya. The Russian production of this charming folk-opera by Mussorgsky, after a tale of the same name by Gogol, was enchanting.

I also managed to get a seat for another ballet performance at the Bolshoi Theatre: again it was *Giselle*! There were many British people in the audience, delegates in some industrial conference. Their wives were pure Betjeman, wearing floor-length frocks and chatting about the British theatre. By a curious coincidence I was sitting behind two ladies who were discussing the recent theatrical season in London, where my adaptation of Friedrich Dürrenmatt's 'black comedy', *The Meteor*, had been presented at the Aldwych Theatre by the Royal Shakespeare Company. I listened eagerly to what the ladies were saying.

'A bit gruesome, dear, don't you think? I thought it was too much of a good thing. A joke's a joke, but that one went on too long.'

'Yes, that's exactly what *I* thought, dear. Now that other one of his—what was it now?—they did it a year or two ago—oh, dear me, my memory's slipping badly, what with the Kremlin tour *and* GUM Department Store all in one day. . . .'

At this point the hubby of the first lady spoke up:

'It was *The Physicists*,' he said. 'Funny sort of play, I thought.'

'That was it! *The Physicists!* Now if you ask me, *that* was much better than *The Meteor*.'

I found myself in complete agreement with them. By an odd coincidence *The Physicists* was playing just then in Moscow, not in my adaptation but in Russian translation. I really had no wish to see it again, so I did not make the effort to get a ticket.

But I saw some brilliant new plays at the small theatres in Mayakovsky Square, including one by the younger dramatist Edward Radzinsky about a disillusioned film producer and his affair with a romantic young girl. I also visited the Operetta Theatre and enjoyed the Satirical Theatre, both on Mayakovsky Square.

In Herzen Street, just past the Moscow Conservatory with its statue of Tchaikovsky, stands the huge Mayakovsky Theatre, which puts on productions of a fairly revolutionary kind. There were some interesting photographic displays of current productions outside, but I could not get a seat. Nor could I see the productions of the Children's Theatre, the Ermolova Theatre and the Arts Theatre, which still has its original auditorium with a seagull painted on the curtain to commemorate Chekhov's play, first performed at this theatre founded by Stanislavsky in 1898. However, I made up for this by a visit to the Stanislavsky Museum, a short walk away in Stanislavsky Street, just off Gorky Street. (The Arts Theatre—to judge by the photographs outside—was presenting a dramatized version of the life of Lenin, which I was not particularly keen on seeing anyhow.) Near the Stanislavsky Museum were the houses where Chekhov and Chaliapin lived, and a little farther on is the enchanting Museum of Folk Art, well worth a few hours.

Another interesting museum in a beautiful red-brick building in Gorky Street was the Museum of the Revolution, where I saw the events of the Revolution movingly displayed in pictures and documents and in a sort of panoramic miniature stage set, with full sound effects. Just beyond stands the small Stanislavsky Theatre and the grand Tchaikovsky Concert Hall, for neither of which I was able to get tickets. I had a good Chinese meal at the Peking Hotel in Mayakovsky Square, with its fine vista down the Sadovaya Ring Road, which encircles central Moscow, the exact centre being the Belfry of Ivan the Great in the Kremlin.

I went back to the Kremlin, to spend a morning looking round the Palace of Arms, one of the oldest museums in Europe: it was Ivan the Terrible who began the collection in the sixteenth century. I went with a conducted tour, on which I met two extremely nice Americans, husband and wife, from New York. They too had been suffering under the Moscow tyranny—they were staying at the same hotel as myself, the Ukraina—and were groaning about the appalling rudeness of the staff. We spent a good deal of time in one another's company, and their wit and charm made the last two days of my stay in Moscow almost bearable.

We had to put on enormous felt overshoes while we were walking round the parquet floors in the Palace of Arms Museum. The American lady giggled infectiously and said:

'We look like zombies.'

I got an almost uncontrollable attack of the giggles, a sort of reaction from nervous oppression. No one else was laughing, and our bespectacled guide, a girl with a very severe face, kept looking at us disapprovingly.

The exhibits were extraordinary in quantity and quality—art fabrics, enamels, silver and gold objects, jewel-encrusted icons and parts of the imperial regalia brought to Moscow from Petrograd at the beginning of the First World War. The displays of decorative embroideries and vestments, furniture and thrones, harnesses and carriages (including the English carriage presented by Queen Elizabeth I to Boris Godunov) were of the greatest interest and beauty. On the second floor is a silver-chandeliered gallery hung with exquisite Gobelins tapestries. This was one of the finest and richest museums I have ever visited.

The time arrived for my departure by Trans-Siberian Railway to Khabarovsk. I had had a lot of trouble with a detestable fat woman in brown, wearing glasses and a forbidding expression, in the service bureau of the Ukraina Hotel. She really put me through the hoop: she was nothing more than a concentration camp wardress. After taking my train tickets she refused to give them back to me until the last minute; whenever I went to see this female *Gauleiter* she barked at me in the most abusive way. I think her nervousness may have been caused by the fact that the desks in the service bureau are connected by hidden microphones with the listening stations on the twelfth floor. Accidentally, as I was sitting down at one of the desks, my foot caught in some electric cord and I found I had pulled out a plug underneath the desk. The girl clerks exchanged uneasy looks. I did not attempt to put the plug in again.

Anyhow, it turned out that instead of having a berth in 'soft class', which I had paid for in Tokyo, I again had to travel 'hard class', sharing a compartment with a man and his very large wife and small child. My heart sank when I realized I should once again have to experience six days of close and uncomfortable confinement. However, farther along the train I saw for the first time the third-class accommodation, which was little better than cattle-trucks with rows of uncurtained bunks. I felt thankful for small mercies after seeing that.

In my carriage every berth was taken except for one compartment which was reserved for one person only—a high-ranking Red Army officer, riding almost in purdah like an Indian bride. He shaved and ate in his compartment and only emerged to go to the filthy, stinking toilet. In my compartment the little girl had her own dark green metal potty (with lid) which she constantly used.

In the next compartment was an attractive woman lawyer from Vancouver, a most intelligent girl. She was sharing her compartment with three Red Army officers. At evening we would sit on the strapontins and chat, gazing out at the mild autumn skies, while we sipped Screwdrivers made from my own special bottle. I was sorry when she got off at Irkutsk.

This time we spent all day skirting Lake Baikal. At a ten-minute stop near the shores of the lake several people in underclothes dashed into the water for a dip from its glittering mica shores. In the twilight skies of Siberia the near-full autumn moon is the colour of dark amber, strung like a paper balloon in the telegraph wires.

My last memory of Russia: the cold, stony faces of young Russian women in uniform at the Immigration and Customs counters at Nakhodka. Their unnaturally pale blue eyes seemed to pierce through and through me, and mentally to undress me. I had nothing to declare but my innocence.

The Japanese returning to their homeland seemed very subdued when I remembered their almost fevered animation on leaving Yokohama. There were no coloured streamers and serenaders at Nakhodka:

the quayside was bare and cheerless. It was a relief when the boat got under way. I was happy to have a first-class cabin all to myself, and I thoroughly enjoyed the trip back to Yokohama. My happiness was almost entirely due to the fact that I was returning to the land I love most of all in the world. But also there had been a subtle change in the staff of the boat. We had exactly the same crew, the same attendants in dining-rooms and bars. But whereas on the trip out they were surly and disagreeable, now they are smiling and sweet. The entire atmosphere of the ship has changed. Why? It is because they are leaving Russia and going for a few days to Japan. They feel a strong sense of relief, as I do, at having left Russia behind.

Waiting for me on the pier at Yokohama were my friends Kyoko Ohara and Tomohiro Yamada. They came armed with authorizations from the university that I should be allowed to land without difficulty. We visited the Immigration Office, where I was most kindly treated by the officers who questioned me about my re-entry permit. It was all the fault of the Intourist department of the Japan Travel Bureau, so I was not to blame in any way. The Immigration authorities told me it would not be necessary for me to go to Hong Kong to arrange a re-entry permit: they would do that for me themselves in Yokohama. I felt a great surge of gratitude towards my Japanese hosts. How different was their treatment from what I suffered in Russia!

As I stepped into the university limousine that was to take me back to my house in Tokyo, I vowed never again to set foot in Russia.

EPILOGUE ON THE TRANS-ASIAN EXPRESS

BUT I am nothing if not inconsistent and inconsequential, and recently I *did* set foot in Russia again. . . .

Japan Air Lines (JAL) and Scandinavian (SAS) both operate services across Russia using great-circle routes. JAL flies once weekly from Tokyo to Moscow using the enormous turbo-prop Aeroflot Tupolev 144's, flown by an Aeroflot crew but with Japanese cabin staff. It is now the swiftest and smoothest way to reach Moscow from Tokyo, and is a most enjoyable flight.

But undoubtedly the more thrilling of these two flights is SAS's twice-weekly hop, skip and jump from Singapore to Copenhagen, with only two stops, at Bangkok and Tashkent. I made this leap through space and time aboard SAS's *Stjold Viking*—the superb Douglas D 6—8 Super-Fan Jet, with an entirely Scandinavian crew. We took off promptly from Bangkok at 10 a.m. and, flying through daylight all the way at Mach ·82, reached Copenhagen on the same day at 5 p.m. (The actual flight time was about eleven hours: the Tokyo–Copenhagen North Pole routes taken by SAS, KLM, JAL and Lufthansa take sixteen hours, with one stop at Anchorage.)

The *Stjold Viking* was soon over Rangoon and the jungle-clad mountains of Burma, then—seat-belts fastened all the way—we had a rather bumpy ride right along the Himalayas (get a window seat on the right-hand side). We drew nearer and nearer to the Himalayas, passed right over Kabul and the Khyber Pass and over the Pamirs, with Samarkand and Bukhara away to our left. The spectacle of the snowy Pamirs and the valleys and deserts of the Hindu Kush is probably the most awe-inspiring in the world. I have flown over the Pole many times, but never felt such horrified admiration as I did for those noble and ghastly ranges of Afghanistan and Uzbekistan.

This brought us across the Russian border—a mere track in a desert waste—and to our landing in Tashkent. The air, when we left the plane for our one-hour 'technical landing', was warm, dry and clear. A handsome, smiling Russian officer collected our passports as we 'deplaned'. The Tashkent airport building, with its tall, noble columns, classical façade and rose gardens, was in the typical thirties style of most Russian railway stations. There were few spectators—only a handful of silent young men gaping at the European girls in miniskirts.

The waiting-rooms were old-fashioned, vast, rather palatial, with chandeliers, mirrors, draped tall windows. Two girls, unsmiling, at the souvenir counter. I purchased some finely embroidered Tashkent skull-caps for dollars, and received American currency in exchange. One can send postcards, but one has to queue to change one's money into roubles first. This takes a long time, so it is advisable to dash straight to the postcard counter, then to go to the souvenir stall and snatch up a few knick-knacks like amber and furs; *starka* and vodka and wines are also sold, as well as *papyrosi*.

Then we were off again—up, up and away across the bleached, parched lands of the Karakoram, straight over the Aral Sea, right across Moscow and Riga with its lovely crescent bays of golden sand. This is the latest way to see Russia, and it is both impressive and boring. After Tashkent, there are landscapes of really unexampled horror—dull, parched, dismal, salt-crusted—but from which I could not turn away my fascinated gaze.

Nevertheless I know that this is not the best way to see Russia. It will always be, for me, the Trans-Siberian Railway!

Index

Abacus, 9
Alcohol, 65
Alexander's Column, 119
Alphabet, Cyrillic, x
Amur River, 18, 22
Angara River, 35, 57
Antimacassars, 41
Archaeology, 119
Art, 'decadent', 90
Atheism Museum, 114
Aurora, cruiser, 117

Baikal, Lake, 35, 152
Baikal, steamer, 1, 3, 4, 12–13
Balakirev, ix
Ballet, 124
—, *Chauve Souris*, ix
—, *Coq d'Or*, x
—, Russe, x
Bath, Somerset, 115
Beatles, 9–10
Beer, 7, 11
Belfrage, Sally, 1, 2
Bolshoi Circus, 13, 50, 54, 67, 68–9
— Opera, 97
— Theatre, 83, 95–6, 99
Bondarchuk, Sergei, 8
Books, 45
Bortsch, 6, 44
Bratsk dam, 34
Brodsky, painter, 114
Buddhism, 48, 139
Bugging, 3, 10, 100, 109, 152
Burgess, Anthony, 2

Catherine II, 112, 114
Caviar, 47, 51, 108
Chagall, Marc, 90
Champagne, 3, 6, 27, 43, 47, 51, 81

Chapiro, Mikhail, 88
Chaplin, Charlie, 47
Chekhov, Anton, ix, 21, 53, 116, 128
Chopin, 147
Chopiniana, 123
Churches, 18, 78, 111, 113, 116, 146
Cinema, 21
Clay, Cassius, 108
Clothing, 23, 31
C.N.D., 65, 110, 141
Coleridge, 29
Communism, 2
Copenhagen, 139
Courtesy, xii, 48
Covent Garden, 124
Currency, 98–9

Dances, 11, 92
Denmark, 139–40
Dertzhavin, Gavril, 114
Diaghilev, x
Dictionary, 45
Djilas, Milovan, 133
Dolgoruki, Yuri, 80
Dostoevsky, ix, 21
Dudinskaya, Natalia, 124

Epilogue, 155–6
Epstein, 25
Esenin, Sergei, 70, 83
Evtushenko, Evgeny, 62, 129; *Mysteries*, 62; *Precocious Autobiography*, 91

Fabergé, 120
Finland, 128, 134–9
Fishing, 15, 22
Flora, 18, 21, 51, 58

INDEX

Fodor, *Guide to Europe*, 1
Fonteyn, 124
Food, 6, 7, 9, 14–16, 27, 33, 43–5, 51, 67, 81, 93, 135, 146–7
— and drink, 8, 27, 43, 47, 97–8, 122, 135
Frost, Robert, 65–6
Fyodorov, Dr Andrei, 46

Gagarin, Yuri, 85
Games, 8
Garbo, Greta, in *Ninotchka*, 12
Germans, East, 16
Gilot, Françoise, 90
Giselle, 99–100, 122, 124, 149
Glazunov, ix
Godunov, Boris, 73, 151
Gogol, ix, 21; *Dead Souls*, 2; *On the Steppes*, 22
Gorky, M., *Childhood*, 133; *Lower Depths*, 2, 45; *Through Russia*, 17, 58, 65; World Literature Publishing House, 46
Gorky Park, 94, 95
— Street, 78, 80, 82
Gregory Fellow in Poetry, ix–x, 25

Hamlet, 139
Harvest, 59
Hastie, *Don't Send Me To Omsk*, 61
Helsinki, 135–7
High Life, Le, 28
Hippies, 14, 20, 23, 27, 38, 47, 51, 73, 108, 137, 139
Horace, 115
How to Behave, xii

Ichikawa, 30
Impressionists, 120
Inefficiency, 19, 78, 106, 153
Innes, Hammond, 30
Intourist, 13, 14, 18, 19, 28, 35, 37, 73, 98, 105, 108
Irkutsk, 56

Iset River, 67
Iya River, 58

January 1905 massacre, 119
Japan, customs, 4
—, islands, 8, 10
—, people, 1–12
— Travel Bureau, x, 37, 41
Jaroslav, 72
Jazz, 93
Journey, return, 143–53

Kamchatka Peninsula, 30
Karlinsky, Simon, 131
Khabarov, explorer, 18
Khabarovsk, ix, 14, 15, 17–21, 25–32
—, Komsomol Square, 31
Kindness, 49
Kirov, 70
— Ballet, 99, 110
Kompot, 6, 45
Kondrashin, Kyril, 88
Koshevnikov, Vadim, xii
Krakow, 147
Kramer, Jacob, 25
Krauts, 145
Kremlin, 82, 151
Krokodil, 45
Kronstadt, 111
Krushchev, 87–8
Kshessinskaya, 117
Kvass, 19, 29, 122

Ladoga, Lake, 134
Landscape, 51
Laughter, 100
Lavatories, 16, 49, 77, 148
Lenin, 9, 14, 19, 20, 38, 108
Lenin Library, 102
Lenin's tomb, 82–5
Leningrad, 105–15

INDEX

Leningrad, Ethnographical Museum, 114
—, Hermitage Museum, 3, 102, 118
— in Second World War, 120
—, window on Europe, 116

MacNeice, Louis, 136
Malaparte, Curzio, 134
Manezhnaya Square, 82
Maps, x
Marriage Italian Style, 30
Marvell, Andrew, 59
Mayakovsky, ix, 84
— Theatre, 150
Melancholia, 132
Mihajlov, Mihajlo, 79
Monastery, Trinity-Saint Sergius, 72
Moscow, 62–81
—, Bolshoi, 3
—, British Trade Fair, xi, 8, 78
— City Hall, 80
—, Congress Building, 96–7
—, Contrasts, 86–93
—, Cosmonauts' Tower, 97
—, Kremlin, 3
— mornings and nights, 94–103
—, mules, 75–81
—, Pushkin Museum, 3
—, skyscrapers, 87
—, subway, 3, 88
—, theatres, 94
—, Tretyakov Gallery, 90
— University, 83, 103
—, winter in, 95
Moskva Hotel, 83
— River, 86
Mosques, 117
Museums, 3, 102, 114, 118, 150
Music, 10, 16, 23, 50, 88
Mussorgsky, 97, 149

Nabokov, Vladimir, 2, 21, 107, 113
Nagel, *U.S.S.R.*, 1
Nakhodka, 8, 11, 12–15
Nativity Boulevard, 80

Neva River, 3, 111–13
Nevsky Prospekt, 113
Newspapers, 45
Niigata, 21
Nijinsky, 124
Novgorod, 107
Novosibirsk, 58, 60
Nureyev, 124

October 1917 revolution, 119
Oistrakhs, 88
Omsk, 53–61
Orwell, George, 131, 142
Ostankino Palace, 87
Ostrovsky, 83

Paintings, 90, 102, 120
Papyrosi, 31, 156
Passion Boulevard, 79
Pasternak, B., 69, 89; *Dr Zhivago*, 63
Pasteur, Louis, 122
Paustovsky, Konstantin, 107
Payne, Robert, 84, 89
Peace, 54
Perm, 68
Peter the Great, 73, 111, 116
Petrodvorets, 3
Philosophy, 42
Photography, 72
Picasso, 26, 90, 102
Piccadilly Circus, 141
Place names, 54
Plakhanov, 113
Poets, 89, 91
—, 'official', 91
Proust, 12, 47, 129
—, *Sodome et Gomorrhe*, 2, 44, 130
Puppets, 99
Pushkin, 3, 79, 112, 114
— Embankment, 95
— Museum, 102

Quarrelling, public, 36

INDEX

Rachmaninov, ix
Railway, Trans-Siberian, ix, xi, 41–53, 156
Red Arrow, 107
Red Square, 84
Reed, John, 85
Repin, 90
Revolution Museum, 150
Rimsky-Korsakov, ix
Rossia Hotel, 87
Russian kindness, 36
— museum, 114
— shrug, 33–9
Russian Verse, Penguin Book of, 2

St Petersburg, *see* Leningrad
Samovar tea kettle, 44, 75
Sandals, 14, 26, 109, 140
Saucers, flying, alleged, 63, 148–9
Sausage, 7
Saveryeva, Ludmila, 8
Scott-Moncrieff, 46
Scriabin, ix, 68
Service, 6, 10, 14, 27, 35, 38, 67, 77, 81, 94, 101, 104, 110, 135, 138, 148, 151
Shilka River, 53
Shops, 33
Shostakovitch, ix, 88, 124
Sibelius, 137; *Swan of Tuonela*, 138
Siberia, 13–24
Sillitoe, Alan, 1, 2
Sleep, 6
Slobodskaya, Olga, 149
Socialist realism, 131
Sokolov, ix
Souvenirs, 31–2, 39, 98
Soviet Literature, 9, 46
Sport, 22, 70
Stalin, 85, 88, 133
Stjold Viking, 155
Stockholm, 138
Stravinsky, ix

Strikes, 38
Students, revolting, 139
Sunday, 29
Suomi, *see* Finland
Sverdlovsk, 67

Tashkent, 155
Tchaikovsky, ix; *Casse Noisette*, 125; *Swan Lake*, 6
Theatres, 83, 94, 95–6, 99, 150
Temple, Shirley, 17
Things foreign, 92
Tokyo, 1, 143–53
— to Moscow non-stop, 50
Tolstoy, ix, 83, 131; *War and Peace*, 8, 79
Tolstoy, son of, 132
Translations, other languages into Russian, 46–7, 89
Tsvetaeva, Marina, 131, 133
Turgenev, ix

Van der Post, Laurens, 1, 2
Vietnam, 55
Vistula River, 146
Vodka, 45, 138, 147
—, Petrovskaya, 98
—, Samovar, 7
—, Stolichnaya, 49, 98
—, Stolovaya, 98, 125
Volga River, 72
Vomitorium, 146
Voznesensky, 92
Vyborg, 134

Waley, Arthur, 46
Warsaw, 144–6
Water, 43
Webern, 88
Wesker, Arnold, 64
Wilson, Harold, 8, 42, 141

Wolfe, Tom, 108–9
World outside, 49–52

Xenophobia, 14

Yasnaya Polyana, 3

Yenisei River, 35
Yokohama, ix, xi, 1, 4

Zagorsk, 3, 72
Zoschenko, Mikhail, 132

C47417